When Life in the Starts Middle

trudy chiswell

◆ FriesenPress

Suite 300 - 990 Fort St
Victoria, BC, V8V 3K2
Canada

www.friesenpress.com

ISBN
978-1-5255-5766-8 (Hardcover)
978-1-5255-5767-5 (Paperback)
978-1-5255-5768-2 (eBook)

1. BIOGRAPHY & AUTOBIOGRAPHY, PERSONAL MEMOIRS

Distributed to the trade by The Ingram Book Company

Dedication

This book is dedicated to my dear friend Rita Springer, who read the initial draft and encouraged, motivated, and gave me the final push to publish. To you, my friend, my thanks are as deep as the deepest ocean. Your encouragement made it possible.

Front Cover

For many years I've been attracted to the hummingbird without knowing why. Recently I came across the meaning attached to the hummingbird in First Nation Folklore, and it resonated deep within me. According to the folklore, the hummingbird teaches you to appreciate and love the miracle of living and helps you focus on the positivity in your life. They are messengers of peace, they heal your body and soul, and they guide you through life's challenges. That really describes my life as you will read in this book. I believe that the symbol of the hummingbird has been God's little messenger of peace from Jeramiah 29:11 in my life.

Endorsements

This quote from trudy's memoir jumped out at me: "I followed that elusive thread of knowledge, because I decided to live life on purpose. There could be no turning back, and it became my belief that it's never too late to seek, to find, to explore, or to discover." The life represented in this book illustrates all of the above. It is lovely and refreshing to read stories of God's redemption in the lives of others. Well done, trudy! Keep walking, running, and learning. But I must tell you that you have graduated from being the "student" and you have become a "teacher" in life for others. Enjoy your success and your continued adventures.

Archdeacon Ron Corcoran
One of trudy's former pastors and author of *Jesus Remember Me*, *The Bishop or the King*, and *Deliver Us from Evil*.

Simply inspirational! Ms. Chiswell's life story is engaging, uplifting, and highly motivational. This book is a must-read for all, and especially for those considering change, no matter how old you are. You will not be disappointed!

Ms. Chiswell is a courageous woman, showing great fortitude and strength against life's adversity in telling the world her story. What a great role model! It is a pleasure having trudy as one of my students.

Richard Wong
Professional Wildlife Artist
Watercolour on Japanese Art Paper

I met trudy chiswell at the launch of my book, "Creating the Impossible – What It Takes to Bring Your Vision to Life," *and soon discovered she was a shining example of its message. That is, it's never too late to follow your heart and realize your dream(s) even if it seems 'impossible.' From graduating from college at age 49, to publishing a book at 75, and so much more, trudy's stories will inspire and encourage you to choose faith over fear, and to "dream new dreams" even when life seems to start in the middle. Thank you trudy for being such as powerful role model of what's possible... at any age.*

Barbara Edie
Best-selling author of *Creating the Impossible*
and transformational coach.

trudy and I were born September 25, 1943. We met September 1958 during our first month in grade nine. I was one of the kids forced to sit for forty-five minutes on a school bus each morning, being brought in from a pretty neighbouring town with peach orchards to gritty Merritton. trudy was a slender, petite girl with a pretty face and thick hair. This is the story of a woman who in the course of seventy-five years came to believe in herself.

Lii Vine
Eyewitness to trudy's life, business woman,
and life-long friend of sixty-one years

I think for most of us teachers, the reason we are in the profession is to help students grow. When trudy went back to school as an adult, she was a shy, insecure, stay-at-home mom with no confidence or skills. Within the Halton Continuing Education Program, and due directly to Don Baker's encouragement and belief in her, she learned that she was not what her parents, siblings, public school teachers, high school teachers, and first husband had told her she was. She could write, she was organized, and she was a wiz at page layout. Don recognized her potential and offered her a job within the program while she was still a student there. She took these skills and new-found confidence and started over. Her life journey, including numerous "opportunities" to start over, is the reason for, and topic of, trudy's book. She has written it expressly to help and encourage anyone who is feeling "stuck." Her book says, "My life has been a scary, exciting, blessed, wonderful journey, and yours can be too." If she isn't the poster child for continuing education, I'm not sure who is.

Wendy Martynuik
Teacher and long-time friend of thirty years

Foreword

The title of this book is so poignant. trudy's life did start *in the middle*, and I had the privilege of getting to know her from *the middle*. She lived with me on several occasions, as she notes in the book, and during these times I got to watch her maneuvre through the many challenges of her life. Through these events, I watched her blossom as a new person. I've been an observer of trudy living life to the fullest, even when she had limited funds and didn't know whether she should live in the west of Canada, where she had a few friends, or in the east of Canada or in Florida, where she had family. She has wrestled with living close to her children as she approached her senior years, or living in a place where she finds personal peace and joy.

trudy has amazed me by the things she has undertaken and the new talents she has demonstrated. She has renovated a home. She has started and managed a successful software company. She has travelled to places in North America in ways that most of us who live here haven't experienced. She is a photographer. She has written travel logs of her trips and many stories. She has learned to paint. And, most importantly, she has listened to the still, small voice of her Lord and waited when she had to wait, and stepped out in faith when she needed to move forward. trudy amazes me.

This book shares the story of how, in her forties, *in the middle*, she realized that she had been held back from becoming all she could be because of insecurities, fear of failure, and lack of confidence in herself. At this middle time in her life, trudy took one step toward a new future of discovering who she really is, and she hasn't looked back. trudy is in her mid-seventies now, and she's still learning new things and planning new adventures.

This book will be a great encouragement, but it will also challenge anyone who believes they're too old to change their circumstances, or not smart enough to learn something new, or too fearful to take a chance on change. trudy's story is told in an easy-to-read fashion. You'll get to know trudy's thoughts and feelings as she tells of her experiences in a wonderfully descriptive way that has the readers feeling like they're at college on the first day of classes or at a celebration with decorations all around them. You will learn how one petite, little lady (who has to take three steps to my one when we go for a walk) stood up for herself and created a wonderful, fulfilled world by herself, for herself.

I hope her story will encourage you to be brave in whatever way you need to be. As you read about trudy's faith, you'll learn that there is a God who created you, and He is someone who has a perfect plan for your life—"plans to prosper you and not to harm you, plans to give you hope and a future." (Jeremiah 29:11). As trudy indicates in this book, this is her life verse and what encourages her to keep on going, no matter what.

Andrea Soberg
Trinity Western University Professor
and long-time friend of thirty years

Introduction

"Don't let others tell you what you can't do. Don't let the limitations of others limit your vision. If you can remove your self-doubt and believe in yourself, you can achieve what you never thought possible."

~ Roy T. Bennett, The Light in the Heart

This is the true story of one woman's journey from dependency and poor self-image to being an independent and enthusiastic adventurer of life. Following the thread of knowledge as a mature student, she became a new person in the process, one step at a time. At forty-two, when her friends were settling down to crafts and bridge parties, she returned to school to get her grade twelve diploma. She went on to get a college degree at forty-nine. At sixty, when those same bridge-playing friends were thinking of grandchildren and a rocking chair, she started her first business. In the twenty-five years since graduating from school, she has become a confident solo traveller who relishes in the adventure of meeting new people. She grew at each mountaintop, but she grew most in the valleys in between.

I am that woman. When my life started in the middle, I chose to be a lifelong learner and to encourage others to reach out and grasp their dreams also—to stretch and experience their potential! Most women of my generation dreamed of being the homemaker of the family, not having a career. Over the past thirty years, I've learned that you're never too old to dream dreams or to set a path to achieve those dreams. I wasn't too old to go to school, travel alone, start a new career, or even a new life. Life had not passed me by! Fear prevented me from doing many things in the first half of my life. Most of all, it kept me from relaxing and taking pleasure in my life. For instance, I enjoyed cooking and wanted to entertain, but the fear of not getting everything perfect had my stomach in knots and my head aching by the time my guests arrived. It all sounds so silly now, but back then it was debilitating. One time we were having the extended family over for one of the children's birthday parties. I cooked for two days to make everything from scratch, even keeping in mind my sister's diet and everyone else's favourites. I prepared dishes of fresh veggies, salads, lovely homemade potato salad, baked ham, and fresh homemade pies.. The table was set perfectly, children all scrubbed and polished to look their best. By the time I got myself ready for the crowd, I was exhausted. By the time the company arrived, the headache was emerging, and by midway through the party, the stomach was starting to complain so much, I couldn't eat all the wonderful food I'd spent so much time preparing. To top it off, all the fresh food I'd prepared for my dieting sister was for nought, as she brought her own food to eat.

During the first half of my life, I lived reactionally to the events and people around me. I was a victim of life with no voice of my own. I lived to please, to meet everyone else's needs and expectations, not even considering what I needed or wanted. Deep down, I think I was afraid of what would happen if I did. Growing into ownership of my own life took many years, and many more before I started acting instead of reacting. That was when life started—in the middle.

My quest to conquer fear began when I was forty-two. It started quite by accident. After a failed first marriage, I had tried again, this time with a wonderful man who was very much like my father in personality. Thirteen years into that marriage, and after being at home with children for twelve years, I wasn't able to go back into nursing—the first field I'd trained for as a teenager—unless I retrained and got re-certified. Looking at other options, I found a part-time job in a bookstore and recognized the need to develop my math skills. I hadn't attended school in twenty-seven years. School had been a terrible experience for me, but I still enrolled in a night school class in 1986. The first night was terrifying! What possessed me to do this voluntarily?

I was the only adult in the room, aside from the teacher. This night school accounting class was mostly made up of high school students who had failed the course and had to take it again. Imagine a large bunch of grade ten fifteen year olds piling into a room, accompanied with lots of noise and laughter. I was more than a little intimidated. Not yet aware of my learning disabilities, I struggled to keep up with the lectures and to complete tests at the same pace as students less than half my age. I learned to read well ahead, to essentially over-prepare for the class. When I finished with a mark of 95 per cent in the class, I was gobsmacked! It gave me courage; I thought maybe I should try another class. That was the first door in an incredible journey toward hope. It inspired me to open the next door, and then the next. Each accomplishment was another brick in the foundation of self-confidence, the ultimate antidote to fear.

At the beginning of this journey, my ultimate accomplishments of post-secondary education, starting a business, and publishing a book, were unthinkable. The journey itself was wrought with many rocks and boulders, seemingly insurmountable at the beginning but possible one step at a time. From that first night school class and over the course of thirty-three years, my life as I knew it turned upside down.

After finishing a draft of this book four years ago, old self-doubt and fear at being transparent reared their ugly heads again, and the book went back to the bottom of the sock drawer. Who was I to use my voice?

Many years ago I read a biography about the Canadian author Robert W. Service and his poem titled "The Cremation of Sam McGee." Service was a bank teller in the Yukon who had written for his personal pleasure since he was a small boy and hidden this writing in the bottom of his sock drawer. At age twenty-six, Service was an active member of the social life in Whitehorse, Yukon and would read his poetry at those events. One day after he had accumulated enough poems, he sent them to his father in Toronto, Ontario to publish. That was the beginning of massive change in his life. That story always encouraged me that perhaps even I, as a late bloomer, could publish my writing.

Today, at seventy-five years of age, I've been a solo traveller of life for twenty-five years and am enjoying every bit of it. I have travelled much, even on my own across Canada for three months, graduated from a three-year college diploma program, started a business at sixty, and then sold it after seven years to provide me with retirement income. After moving to Florida to be near my daughter's family, I completely renovated a house and flipped it. There's apparently a first time for everything. Then, when I realized that the cost of the US medical system wasn't financially sustainable for me, I moved to the other side of Canada to live in a part of the country that spoke to my soul—Victoria, on Vancouver Island, British Columbia. There I discovered I could make close friends no matter where I landed.

Life is too precious to moan, complain, or be miserable, so I treasure every moment. Life for me as a senior is not a time to sit and wait to die, but a time to throw myself into the community in volunteer work. It's a time to give back and enjoy it. Not having to worry anymore about earning a living, retirement is when I can do what I want to do in life. Learning to do water colour painting on Japanese art paper for the first time in my life at seventy-four, I carried on and just finished showing my paintings in a gallery at seventy-five. I'm loving life and all it holds!

This is the story of how I got here.

Building Sandcastles

"You are never too old to set another goal or to dream a new dream."

~ C.S. Lewis

Have you ever built a sandcastle? Once, when I was a child, I spent a lazy afternoon at my favourite vacation spot on the shores of Lake Erie enjoying the beach with my parents. Close to the water's edge, on the cool, hard-packed sand, I built my castle of dreams. Spiralling turrets shot up into the sky. A shell stood proudly as the flag, and a little bridge traversed the moat. Finally, feeling I was quite finished, I stood back to admire what I had created. I congratulated myself on a job well done!

But a sense of dismay set in when I saw a storm brewing out on the lake. Dark, purple clouds rolled in, and when the wind picked up, water began lapping against my castle. The storm blew in quickly, and I was horrified to see big waves swelling closer and closer. Soon they engulfed my lovely castle of dreams ... and it was no more. I had built on sand without a firm foundation. This event became an analogy of the first half of my life.

I built sandcastles of dreams without putting in the effort or using the materials that would make them real. I was forty-two years old before I realized that life was a "do-it-yourself" proposition. Up until then, I'd allowed storms of adversity to destroy my dreams, and I felt powerless to do anything about it. Everyone seemed smarter, more significant, or stronger than I was. I'd spent my time searching for something I could never seem to grasp, never quite putting it together, never quite fitting in, and always striving to be accepted. I was much older than forty-two when I stopped doing that.

I grew up in what I assumed was an average family—I was the youngest of three daughters—my parents instilled in us to respect others, have integrity, and practice high work ethics. Mom and Dad were both introverts, and when it came to affection, we were not a demonstrative family—a characteristic I craved for and chose to change in my own family in the future, thanks to a brother-in-law who came into the extended family and gave hugs lavishly. Ray was a hugger!

Dad was a good man, a man of few words but kind and gentle with his family. Dad had gone back to school as an adult to get an education in order to work in a bank; later, I'd follow in his footsteps, at least the part about going back to school. After having three girls he decided to move us all from Coniston, Ontario down to Southern Ontario so we would have a better future. There wasn't much for women up north except being a homemaker during that period of time.

The move was a sacrifice for him, as he then had to find work in a paper mill for better pay. An amazing mathematician, he sacrificed his own preference in work to provide a better life for his girls. He was also frustrated with his three girls, who struggled with numbers. I remember my dad being able to mentally add up any four-digit numbers we would give him. By the time we got to the end of the list of numbers, he would have the answer. Amazing! I guess we were all late bloomers, because my sisters and I all became good at bookkeeping in later years. We all did the budget and books in our families.

I loved Dad dearly, and I suppose I'm much like him as an introvert. Being the youngest in the family, I followed him around like a puppy when he went on his part-time job hanging curtains.

Mom was a gentle soul. She was a dressmaker, a talent learned from my Grannie Daley, who was a tailoress by trade before she married. Mom was a hard worker as a clerk in a grocery store and then a fabric store all her life to make ends meet for her little family. Even so, she still made time to make most of the clothes and wedding dresses for her girls.

To say that school was a challenge for me is an understatement! I struggled with spelling all the way through school and just barely made it through each grade. Marks for spelling were taken off everything in every subject, so my marks were always low. I'm sure if they could have taken spelling marks off finger painting, they would have. I barely scraped through grade ten. I hated school, and it hated me!

Is it any wonder that I thought I was a dummy? It took me half my life to get over this misconception. I'm sure this is where my poor self-image was rooted. School was such a struggle for me that I couldn't wait to get out, so at sixteen I told my dad that I wanted to leave school. "Well," he said, "I can't stop you, but you need some kind of trade to get a job. Why have more education? You'll just marry and stay home to raise a family."

Most women of my generation and social economic position—the working middle-class—were trained to think when we were adults, we'd each replicate our mother's lifestyle. There were few careers open to us; you could either be a secretary, a nurse, or a teacher. Very few parents thought of post-secondary education or careers for their daughters. Even the rich who sent their daughters to post-secondary or finishing schools imagined their daughters marrying, staying home to raise a family, and doing volunteer work. It was a peculiar time of horrid polyester bell bottom pants, miniskirts, vinyl floors, and vinyl 78 records. It is rather comical to realize I've now lived long enough to see most of that come back in fashion.

Being a passive teenager, I didn't question my father, but internally I was frustrated with the options and didn't know how to express my feelings. I saw that there was a ten-month nursing assistant course in Hamilton, Ontario, which meant I would at least get away from home.

So when I was seventeen I travelled, terror-filled, to Hamilton to go to nursing school. In those days, Hamilton was a soot-filled, smelly, industrial city of steel mills, half an hour from my childhood home of Merritton, a small town that stank with sulphur from the paper mills. Living at the downtown YWCA in Hamilton, I had to wipe the soot off the window sill every few days to avoid getting soot on my uniform. I trained as a Registered Nursing Assistant (equivalent to today's Licensed Practical Nurses, LPNs). The year-long program was open to anyone who had completed grade ten, which I had ... barely. After training, I wanted to move to Western Canada but never pursued the dream because of fear. Instead, I married at eighteen to the first person who asked me.

In 1962 I was married to Jim, just shy of my nineteenth birthday. The marriage was a disaster from the day of the wedding. I was only eighteen years old and simply fell into the relationship. There was a lack of maturity and communication in our relationship. I remember thinking how grown up we were. What a laugh! At nineteen we were catapulted into parenthood at the end of our first year of marriage when our son Dennis was born. I remember feeling so grown up at the time, but I was just playing the part. Seeing my own youngest child years later at eighteen years old, I realized with shock how young and naïve I'd been. I couldn't imagine my daughter following my path. Thank goodness she didn't!

Our daughter Cherie was born two years later in 1965. Cherie was a sweet, quiet baby who never caused any problems. She was so quiet that if I sat her in a corner to play, she was still there an hour later. We never realized until much later that she suffered from medical and delayed-development problems. Cherie has struggled with issues all her life, but she never complained and always made the best of her situation whatever life threw her way. I am proud of her courage to make the best of her life.

There was only one book, Dr. Spock, on how to raise children at that time; otherwise, most of us relied on our parents to guide us through the child rearing days. The attitude at the time when my son Dennis was born was "If Mom did it and Grandma did it, it must be good enough for our children." Half my life was lived as a replica of my mother. In the early 1970s, women's lib hit the stage, and everything changed. At first it didn't affect my life and I remained a replica of my mother. In the second half of my life, I finally experienced liberation, but for now I was still the obedient little wife.

When people dismissed me from conversations with statements like, "You don't really understand the situation," I accepted it as my due. The youngest child of three daughters, I learned to take on the role of "youngest" no matter how old I was. Many people in my life felt free to tell me I didn't know what I was talking about. I never had a statement or original thought I could claim as my own. I qualified all my input into conversations with, "John says" or "Sally says."

I don't blame these people for my poor self-image, because I allowed and accepted their assessment of me as the truth. I was surrounded by passive-aggressive people and was naive about how to fight back. Until the age of forty-two, I lived as a victim to others' assessment of me. I assumed I had no voice of my own, and it took me decades to find it.

Full-time work, parenthood, and poor communication were too much for my first marriage. After three years and two children, when the problems within the marriage came crashing down on me, I had a complete breakdown and was diagnosed with clinical depression. That was the beginning of years of chronic depression for me.

Depression is such a terrible malady. I felt like someone had thrown a wet blanket over me, and it was hard to even raise an arm or get out of bed. It was like wearing a pair of sunglasses indoors, making the whole world look dull, or like I was in the bottom of a deep, black pit with no light at the end of the tunnel. I lost all hope! Depression is a chemical imbalance in the body, and I got tired of hearing people say, "Just pull up your boot straps and get on with life." I had no control over what was happening to me and had to wait for the drugs to run their course. Once diagnosed with clinical depression, I had to wait for the medication to help once it got into my system. Some people seemed to think I had a choice in whether to be depressed or not. Thank goodness there have been tremendous advances in the acceptance and treatment of people with depression.

I'll never forget the day my dad came to help me pack up my belongings. The sun caressed the trees that burst forth with new life. Crocuses bloomed in a garden where I was digging up yellow daffodils, also in bloom. I carefully transferred them to a red clay pot. Sadness overwhelmed me!

Sitting on the front step, my father watched me dig up bulbs planted only last fall. His eyes looked so sad. I know now that my dad grieved for his daughter. I was so consumed with my own agony, I failed to see the pain in my father's eyes. It was as if in digging up the bulbs, I tried to claim a fragment of life from my shattered marriage.

My marriage had not been one of flying dishes or flying words. Instead, it contained little or no communication, the silence like a pressure cooker. Marrying at the young age of eighteen and catapulting immediately into motherhood and work had left no time or energy for meaningful communication. One day the marriage could take no more pressure. So great was the breakdown in communication that three weeks before this incident, when I was admitted to the hospital and subsequently diagnosed with clinical depression, my husband had no idea of any problem. But the relationship had shattered!

Now I sat on the ground, digging up my precious yellow daffodils, feeling confused, lost, and a failure. Where was the "happy ever after" marriage I'd always dreamed of? How strange the things I felt I needed to take when I moved out—taking the babies' diapers out of the rinse water and packing them in a plastic bag to dry later, packing my good china in a box and gathering together the rest of my few possessions from before the marriage. As Dad loaded three years of my life into the car, my tears fell on the daffodils.

During the separation, I lived with and had the support of my family, but my self-confidence was nonexistent. I wanted to go back to work, but I didn't think anyone would hire me because of the stigma of clinical depression. At that time any mental illness was a hush-hush condition, never talked about in polite company. As a nurse, I had worked in the Hamilton Psychiatric Hospital for a year, so I knew the perception well.

It was my father's encouragement that enabled me to get back into the workforce. With my training as a Registered Nursing Assistant, I think my father thought if I got back to work, I'd be able to be independent and pull out of the depression. A psychiatrist helped me climb out of the hole. I began to take ownership of my life in small ways, but it didn't happen overnight. It took six months. They were baby steps, but eventually I could get up in the morning, dress, and take the children for walks. I'm amazed at what my parents put up with during that time and their patience with me.

It was many months of counselling and many months of talks before our little family was able to come together again to try to resolve our differences. My marriage was worth a second chance. The daffodil bulbs returned to their garden, but the connection was tentative. I went from my family doctor to a marriage counsellor and finally to a psychiatrist to try to save the marriage. Nothing worked.

In 1969, four years after the separation, my father died. Dad went into the General Hospital in St. Catharines with a massive heart attack, and my husband and I went to visit him the day he died. As I approached his bed, Dad looked at me with those sad eyes, and I knew in my heart that he was telling me to stand up and be strong, to stop allowing people to take advantage of me and to take responsibility for my actions. He had known my husband was unfaithful to me before I did. I looked into his eyes, and I knew I couldn't pretend anymore.

Dad's death cemented my resolve to do something to improve my situation. I decided to leave my marriage and make a life for my children. After seven years together, my marriage had shattered, and it couldn't be put back together. The lesson from this experience caused me to instill in my children to wait until they were older to marry. It's a rare teenager who has the maturity to handle marriage and babies while working—and survive!

The positives that came out of the marriage were my two children. They were the reason I got up each day. The final separation and then divorce was ugly, and I was deeply wounded. I expected to work for the rest of my life and never marry again. Many years later, my first husband came and asked forgiveness for his unfaithfulness and the part he played in the failure of the marriage, but at the time, nothing about the situation felt resolved or okay. My parents had enjoyed a solid and good marriage. I believed the myth that everyone got married and lived happily ever after. When it didn't happen for me, I felt like a failure. My castle of dreams lay shattered at my feet.

From Darkness to Light

Then Jesus again spoke to the people, he said, "I am the Light of the world. Whoever follows me will never walk in the darkness, but will have the light of life."

~ John 8:12,

Fate had other things in store for me. For a year I worked and raised my children on my own, as I had planned. I was a nurse at Joseph Brant Hospital in Burlington, Ontario. Dennis and Cherie were six and four respectively. Although I didn't know it at the time, this was my first tentative, shaky step into living life intentionally. Living alone brought up so much anxiety for me that my mind would race with imagined worst-case scenarios. For instance, I knew my ex had a rifle. Although he'd never threatened me physically, every time I heard the cherry banger go off in the orchard to chase the birds from the cherry trees, I was afraid that it was my ex coming after me. I realize now that my ex would never have done that, but at the time it was agonizing torture.

A year later, I met a man I knew casually through friends. He was a gentle soul who provided helpful support for what I was going through and paid sincere attention to my children. My knight in shining armour! He reminded me very much of my father with his quiet, gentle spirit. Over the next year, much to my surprise, I found myself in love for the first time in my life.

Two years later, in 1972, we married, and our daughter was born the following year. For the next eighteen years our life together was everything I thought marriage was about. Ralph was a supportive, loving father and husband who didn't want me to have a job outside the home. Instead, I worked hard to be the best wife and mother I could, but the chronic depression was like a cloud that haunted me once again after our daughter was born. After Melody's birth, I suffered with postpartum depression. Staying at home, I did all the mommy things, like preparing homemade meals and baking cookies and bread—all with a spotless house. We grew all our vegetables in our first home and, following my mother's footsteps, I canned everything we grew.

Still suffering with mild depression when Melody was about four, I talked to my husband about me going away to a retreat centre up in Northern Burlington for a few days. I just knew I needed to get away. Sometimes when driving the car, I would think, *If I just swerve in front of that truck, it will be over.* But then I would look over at my daughter and decide I couldn't do it. Something powerful was looking after me at that time.

Many people would never have known I suffered with chronic depression, because I was very good at wearing the public mask. It frustrated me, because I felt I had no reason to be depressed. I had a wonderful husband, three great children, and a new home in the country. Life was perfect! My sandcastle was complete.

In February of 1978 when I got to the retreat centre, I walked for miles and miles in the snow—so much so that the staff, who had been informed that I was suffering from depression, were getting worried about me.

One day I walked to the top of a small hill at the back of the centre, where I saw a little bench. I thought I'd never reach the top. When I got to the top, which really was a very little hill, I could see the country for miles. I sat there for a long time and finally cried out to God, "If you don't give me everything you've got, I will never make it down this hill."

I felt an incredible peace envelop me. I was bundled up with a scarf and mittens, but after the long walk I had been shivering and chilled through. Suddenly it felt like warm water was poured all over me, and I felt so light, it felt as if I could fly. I flew off that hill to talk to the pastor and accept Christ. I didn't fully understand what this meant, but I saw something in the people here that I knew I needed. He prayed with me and that was the beginning of an incredible journey that changed my life. I became a born again Christian. It felt like someone had picked me up and turned me around 180 degrees. The depression left me instantly.

With the depression gone, I started volunteering at Melody's school when she was in kindergarten. I was also growing as an individual now and read self-help books veraciously. This was quite a difference from when I was in school and had trouble reading. It was a miracle in itself. The teachers had always put on all my report cards, "trudy needs to read more." Being able to read so much now was part of the healing that took place, and I had a desire to be a better me.

Ralph and I were so caught up in the life of our children that there was never time for just the two of us to talk about our feelings or dreams. Our conversation was always about the problems with the children. The oldest two were a challenge, but Ralph was amazingly patient and calm with them.

Before our marriage I had gone to a psychiatrist to sort out the depression and the problems of the first marriage. I didn't want to see a repeat of that happening this time, so after thirteen years together, I spoke to Ralph about my feeling that we needed to see a marriage counsellor. His response was that he didn't have any problems.

Because of my poor self-image, my reaction to his statement was that it must be me that had the problem, and I needed to fix it. But how? Because my youngest was now twelve, I thought that perhaps getting a part-time job would "fix" me. I acquired a job as a clerk in a bookstore, which led me to consider taking a night school course in accounting. I was starting to feel a little better about myself and thought that perhaps a night school course would help me with math at work. After my experience growing up, I was excited and terrified at the same time to go into a school again.

Ralph encouraged me to go back to school, thinking it would help me with my poor self-image. Up to this point in my life, I thought I was truly a dummy. I thought everyone was smarter than me and had it more together. If there was an important decision to make, I'd always go to someone for advice, because I didn't trust my own thought process. This image was reinforced by my family, who would tell me I didn't know what I was talking about on numerous occasions. Years later, after the paradigm shift in my life, I realized that I did have a brain in my head and I did know what I was talking about. But not yet. Ralph also had little education, so he constantly motivated me to keep going through the process, helping with meals and housecleaning so I could study. He was a great encourager.

It appeared that I had a perfect life. A new sandcastle was complete.

However, appearances were deceptive, as I was still living reactionally to events and people around me. I still had poor self-image and no clear voice of my own.

It's difficult to be this transparent in a book, but it sets the stage to see the incredible transformation my life took and the work God did in my life. A door to a different life was before me, and I had no idea how it would change me. The journey begins.

Not long after I started night school, I was in the 100 *Huntley Street* building in Burlington, which has a huge stained glass window in its courtyard. I closely examined the bright pieces of red, yellow, and pale blue. The light made them sparkle and glitter. The sun shone through the transparent pieces, and I could see the little garden outside. Then I noticed the dark brown, deep burgundy and the royal purple pieces of the window. The dark pieces weren't particularly pretty to look at that closely; the sun didn't make them sparkle, and I couldn't see through them. From the largest piece of glass to the tiniest piece, they were all held together by strong lead that was bent around each piece to make it fit perfectly. Without the strength of the lead, the window would not exist.

Only as I stood back from the window was I able to see the beautiful picture that all of the pieces of coloured glass made up. There was a large, open hand with kingly robes around the wrist, reaching down to a small, worn hand stretching up. The small hand barely touched the fingertips of the large, open hand. The bright, sparkly pieces of glass still sparkled, and the transparent pieces of glass still allowed the sun to stream into the room, but it was the dark pieces of glass that caught my attention. They gave the whole picture depth and beauty! Without the dark pieces, the picture would have been flat and uninteresting.

Without the lead that fit perfectly around each piece of glass, all of the pieces would have fallen and smashed into a thousand tiny fragments on the floor. Without the lead holding the pieces together, I couldn't have admired the beauty of the whole picture.

At that moment, I had the lead of my faith in God holding me together. I had dark pieces inside myself that I still didn't understand, and I had the sparkly, transparent pieces of a new desire and willingness to learn.

Out beyond this window and the courtyard of the *Huntley Street* building, the door of a new life was opening, and I had no idea how much my stepping through it was going to change me.

A Most Unlikely Student

Night School at Forty-Two

Be strong and courageous. Do not be afraid; do not be discouraged,
for the Lord your God will be with you wherever you go.

~Joshua 1:9

In my early life, my own fear had barred many doors to discovery, and it took great courage to push through such a door to experience the other side. Those first steps took all my energy and courage.

A successful experience in my night school accounting class encouraged me to try a grade ten English class a few years later. This time I dragged Ralph along for support. He was enrolled in the same class with me but didn't share my passion for learning.

It was 1985 and Jean Baker, the teacher, was returning a short story we'd handed in the previous week. A petite lady with dark hair, Jean was an energetic teacher who inspired her students. As she came up the row and handed me back my story, I stared at it in confusion. This couldn't possibly be mine! Seeing an English paper in front of my face with an A on it just didn't compute.

Suddenly, I realized that Jean was talking to me. "Have you ever considered a career in writing?" she asked.

Well, that was so ridiculous from my experience at school, I literally laughed in her face. What a ludicrous statement! I told her she couldn't be serious, because I couldn't spell.

She then proceeded to explain about learning disabilities and said that it wasn't a measure of intelligence to have a learning disability. It only meant that teachers hadn't taught me in the way I needed to learn.

This was a revelation to me. When I was in school, there was no recognition of learning disabilities. There were the smart students, the strugglers, and the dummies. Most classes were lectures, and I hadn't learned yet that during a lecture I needed to take notes and then type them out in order to capture the lesson of the lecture. So I struggled, and I felt like a dummy.

One year after Jean's class when I was in my mid-forties, I took an aptitude test before going into college. I was shocked when it came back that I had above average intelligence, and Jean Baker's explanation to me that a learning disability is no measure of a person's intelligence became a reality in my life.

Jean must have seen something in me that I didn't see in myself. She kept encouraging me to write, write, write. It soon became an addiction. Each week I would find little notes of encouragement on my work. This gave me further courage to become more transparent in my writing. A thesaurus and dictionary now became my constant companions as I wrote. Like Robert W. Service, the famous poet of the Klondike Gold Rush time, I had been a closet writer for many years. I didn't hide my writing under my socks like he did, but it was certainly at the bottom of a drawer so that no one would find it or by accident read it. Writing was my own private world, a part of me that I was afraid to share.

Jean was special. I don't think she even recognized her gift for encouraging people who had a negative school history. Many have this opportunity, but few take up the challenge. Jean unlocked my dreams, allowed me to expand my horizons, and gave me courage to set new goals and dream new dreams. How thankful I am that one teacher took the time to support a most unlikely student. She changed my life. No one had ever encouraged me like this before.

On class days, I'd hurry home from work in the bookstore and give my family a rushed supper. Ralph and I would pile into the car, and off we'd go to Lord Elgin High School for our class with Jean. Clutching my notebook with my latest writing endeavour, we'd walk down the long hallway and slide into our seats on the far side of the room—not too close to the front in case we got asked a question! We were still cautious. I was amazed that I was still capable of learning something new even at forty-two. The more I used my brain, the more I was capable of learning.

Learning went on every day in my life from that moment forward. My brain had not gone to mush. Amazing! Going back to school had tapped an unknown reservoir of possibility in me. It felt like looking through a telescope and seeing a far horizon, one I didn't know was there but perhaps could get to with some effort. I had never in my life experienced this feeling.

Job Hunting

"Many of life's failures are people who did not realize how close they were to success when they gave up."

~ *Thomas A. Edison*

I worked at the bookstore part-time for two years before being laid off because of cutbacks. Now it was 1986, and with a little more confidence than before, I started working and going back to school, and I was thrown into job hunting mode, another new experience for me. At the time I graduated from nursing school, you just decided the hospital you wanted to work in, applied, and got the job. Since I was already enrolled in night school, I didn't have the time or desire to update my nursing training, so I explored other possibilities. Working in a school helping others seemed a good marriage of my desire to learn and my need of a job. But how I dreaded the interview process!

After a number of interviews, I exclaimed, "I'm not going for another interview. They're demoralizing and nerve-wracking, and I've had enough!" Famous last words as I drove back one Tuesday afternoon from my most recent job interview. I had only been home a few hours when I got a phone call from a school principal. He asked if I was still interested in a job as a teacher's assistant.

Interested? Yes! I thought this was the type of job I really wanted, but that meant another interview the next day.

I found the school in plenty of time and entered the school office. Sitting down with the principal and vice-principal, I tried deep breathing to relax. The principal began to describe the child I would work with. I couldn't believe my ears! It was as if they were describing my oldest daughter when she was this boy's age. I'd be working one on one with Billy, a grade eight boy with emotional problems and learning disabilities. I became excited as they described the boy and my duties, because I felt I had something to offer from my life experience. I couldn't get this boy out of my head when I went home. The job felt right.

After the interview, the nail-biting anxiety began. I waited impatiently beside the phone for an acceptance or rejection.

Later, on a beautiful sunny day, my mood was dark and cloudy, as I heard I wouldn't be working with Billy. It wasn't as though my whole world had come to an end, but I found job interviews and rejections taxing, as my emotions went up and down like the elevator in the CN Tower. One minute I would be positive about the future, and the next I would plummet to the depths of insecurity.

That's it! I'm not going for another job interview! I said to myself … again. Despite Jean's positive input in my night school English class, my self-confidence at this point was still pretty shaky, and the rejection of job hunting overwhelmed me like a tsunami wave.

It was only a few hours after this famous statement that the phone jingled again. Another interview request, and another time I rallied my courage and tenacity to try again. Something in me couldn't give up. So off I went, armed with all the self-confidence

I could muster. During the interview, the job sounded perfect. Again! I waited to hear while others were interviewed.

A call came saying the interview went well but the job had been given to someone else. It was like hearing the doctor say, "The surgery was a success, but the patient died."

Another rejection was followed by another invitation to interview. The cycle continued. After so many rejections from "perfect jobs," I finally learned to keep my information private until it was a sure thing. Early on in my job hunt, I had shared every call for an interview with anyone who walked across my path, and then when it didn't pan out, I had to answer all those, "How did it go?" questions. Having to say I didn't get the job made me feel like a failure, and I assumed others were judging me because of it. That wasn't necessarily true, but my self-confidence was like a roller coaster at this point.

Finally, an opportunity came to get off the roller coaster. I was called for an interview with the Halton Board of Continuing Education, and off I went, carrying my resume and references with as much confidence as I could fake. As I entered another office building, the sun beamed brightly through the windows. The positive vibes were flowing! It felt like another positive interview, and Don Baker, the director, just happened to be the husband of my beloved teacher, Jean.

As I left the office, I practised my mantra, "Something wonderful is going to happen to me today!" At that time, I was listening to *Seven Habits of Highly Effective People* by Steven Covey to boost my self-image. I tried to keep a positive outlook that eventually I would find a job. This time, success. I got the job.

> *"Live out of your imagination, not your history."*
> ~ *Stephen Covey*

A quiet, unassuming man, Don Baker had a vision to enable adults to achieve their grade twelve diploma in a daytime setting, which I became a part of. As director of continuing education, Don hired me to help promote the new daytime Adult Learner Program, where I eventually became a student after my night school classes. It was rather a strange arrangement and unique opportunity to be marketing a program for adults while being one of the students. However, because I talked to people from the heart of where I was, they could identify with me.

I took photos of students in classes, created a display, and then took it to many of the local malls. I remember one lady coming up to me and sharing how difficult school had been for her and that she didn't think she was smart enough to go back to school. When I shared my story of the same experience, it encouraged her to go and register. She was in the first graduating class with me.

During my job search, I'd heard that it could take fifty to a hundred job applications to get a position. I don't know how many resumes I sent out at that time, but the trick was not to give up! With the ups and downs, a positive mental attitude was sometimes difficult to maintain. I needed to adjust and readjust many times before I grasped the prize, and I discovered that I had more determination, tenacity, and belief in myself than I'd ever imagined.

Craving More

"*The most difficult thing is the decision to act, the rest is merely tenacity. The fears are paper tigers. You can do anything you decide to do. You can act to change and control your life; and the procedure, the process is its own reward.*"

~Amelia Earhart

Soon it wasn't enough just to go to night school; I was eager to finish my grade twelve diploma. With the ongoing support of Ralph, and after getting clearance from my employer, I began day school in the mornings, threw my textbooks in the car at noon, changed my shoes, and went to work in the afternoon, marketing the Adult Learner Program, in which I was also a student. Later in life, I wished I still had that kind of energy.

I felt like a woman with three hats. In 1986, when my children were twenty-three, twenty-one, and thirteen, there was my wife and mommy hat, my student hat, and my professional hat. Before I started to balance these three aspects of my life, I felt trapped inside a room of other people's expectations. It was a challenge! I felt the family front had to be perfect, and I wanted to be perfect as a student and in the job. But going to school and the new job felt like someone had thrown open a door to my life, and fresh air poured in. It was exhilarating.

The professional hat was probably the most difficult for me to wear at this point because of my lack of self-confidence and the response of those who knew I didn't have a university degree. I didn't have the confidence at this point to develop a plan and proceed without first checking it out with someone I saw as having more authority than me. Some people I worked with equated intelligence with a piece of paper and thought it ludicrous that I would have the audacity to attempt what I was doing. Creating and developing a marketing plan and talking to potential students was intuitive to me, and because I was a mature student, I knew which advertisements and promotions appealed to prospective mature students.

On the home front, I still kept the place spotless, cooked the meals, and baked cookies. Many years later, my daughter Melody told me that my generation had ruined it for her generation. We did everything—the volunteer work, school, work, and still kept the family home as if we didn't work. Melody and I chuckled over that, but there was always a cost for all of that effort that we didn't let others see. We were the flux generation, in between the expectation of being a replica of our mothers' lifestyle and women's lib. It took our daughters' generation to settle into the new mould and realize that we couldn't, or didn't, have to be super-moms.

I continued to follow the elusive thread of knowledge through the winter of 1986 and was fortunate to have two more teachers who made an impact on my life and helped me to grow further. My grade twelve teacher, Marilyn, became my mentor and dear friend beyond the school walls. She encouraged and prodded me to keep focused on my dream to stretch beyond the current reality. Marilyn challenged my mind by continually encouraging me to keep pressing on in my math problems. When I couldn't get adding percentages, Marilyn came and sat beside me to show me step by step until I got it. What a treasure! Each time I conquered another type of math problem, another brick was established in my wall of confidence.

Math in school had always been a challenge for me. I managed, but it was not my favourite subject, and it didn't help that my father had been an accomplished mathematician. With Marilyn teaching, I finally got it. There was the old cultural notion that girls weren't good at math or science, subjects perceived to be a man's area of expertise. Thankfully that notion has been shattered and we now realize that women can also be excellent in both.

All her students loved Marilyn. She demonstrated a deep concern for us all. Many times she would be off in a corner helping a student through a difficult time. Adults bring to the classroom unique problems because of their work and family schedules, as well as negative memories of school from childhood. On the plus side, they also bring the lessons of life experience to the classroom. Marilyn recognized the adult students' liabilities as well as their virtues. She encouraged each one of us to reach our potential. Most importantly, she had faith in us when we had no faith in ourselves.

As an adult, I was lucky when it came to teachers—so different from the ones I'd had in my teens. I only remember one caring teacher when I was in grade ten and had failed science. Knowing that I was going on to take nursing training, he said, "I know that you understand the material, so I'm going to give you a verbal test." With that encouragement, I got a passing grade to be able to go on to the nursing program. Otherwise, as a teenager, I felt stranded when it came to school.

Now, all of these years later, I had Pat as my grade twelve English teacher. She had a gentle, quiet nature and a nervous, infectious laugh. After I handed in a story I had written about my grandmother, Rose, and her death compared to the blooming rose garden outside her window, Pat encouraged me to keep writing. Even after I graduated, she'd call me every so often to see how I was doing. Pat demonstrated a rare kind of caring—consistent, and a step beyond the expected.

As I worked toward my diploma, I found our classroom to be a comical place. These were the early days of adult education in a day school setting. The program was not yet a year old, and it had been difficult to find schools willing to provide precious space to adults. We were housed in a technical school that was bursting at the seams with students. The only available space was on the school's stage. There were a few scraggly rows of odd desks and an old teacher's desk that looked like it had been salvaged from the back storage room. A blackboard had been attached to the back wall of the stage with a bulletin board off to one side. Marilyn always looked for cheerful posters to put up on the bulletin board to motivate us. I remember one poster of a small kitten hanging on for dear life to the handle of a basket of flowers. The quote was, "Hang in there!"

Occasionally the school would need the stage for normal school activities, and we'd be evicted from our little corner. So off we'd go to another classroom, with teachers carrying large bags of textbooks. All eighteen students and two teachers looked like a convention of ladies on a mission as we traipsed down the hall! These teachers made us see the funny side of the whole drama, and we all felt very privileged to be part of it.

The winter flew by! It was like eating popcorn during an exciting movie—before I knew it, I had reached the bottom of the box. The term was at an end! Was the goal the grade twelve

diploma, or just learning and growing our brains? School was ,
enriching, so truly educational, the diploma was no longer the
point. The point was the experience of tapping the previously
unrecognized well of knowledge and the positive reinforcement
we all received, some of us for the first time in our lives.

I had accepted the challenge to go through the door of knowledge and found out knowledge is power. No one could take that
away from me. I was building a firm and lasting foundation, one
of self-confidence and hope—one brick at a time.

Running ... Running everywhere..
The shoes take time
and strike a pose
The pace ....
was crashing
much too fast
I missed
my brother
walking
past!

Trudy Bridle

I wrote this poem and drew this image after a dear friend died suddenly while I was running flat out getting an education at college and missing spending time with her. Marie was one of my encouragers who is sadly missed.

It's Never Too Late

Nothing is impossible. The word itself says "I'm possible"!

~ *Audrey Hepburn*

While preparing for a graduation in June of 1987 was very exciting, at the same time fear raised its ugly head. During the process of preparing for the ceremony and decorating the room, I got very quiet in the office while trying to focus on what needed to be done and not show the staff the fear that consumed me. It took the head secretary of continuing education asking me, "Are you okay?" to bring me back to reality and calm down. Ultimately, I refused to give in to the fear. By the end of the ceremony, I was wrung out and exhausted, but it was a good exhaustion ... another block established in the foundation of confidence! I discovered that courage isn't the absence of fear; it's feeling fear and persevering to the other side in spite of it.

It could have been any high school graduation, in any high school auditorium. There were the paper flowers, life-sized silhouettes hung behind the podium, and family members in their suits and Sunday dresses waiting impatiently. A newspaper reporter had come to interview these pioneer graduates. It was a glorious June day with warm weather and a bright, sapphire blue sky. The eighteen students waiting nervously in the lounge could have been any graduating class. But they weren't! This was my county's first graduating class of the daytime Adult Learners Program.

Graduates filed into the room, and proud families beamed at their special person in the graduation line. As diplomas were handed out, old fashioned camera flashbulbs popped and crackled. Digital cameras were invented in 1986 by Nikon and would change our whole experience of taking photos. Each graduate knew this accomplishment was a community effort. We were the pioneers! The experience built self-esteem in each one of us and opened the door to new vistas. The air felt electrified! The event was like the birth of a new baby, and this was delivery day. Teachers and management had planned and anticipated the development of this program over long meetings for years; this was the first fruit of their labour.

I was nervous and excited on two fronts: one as a student and at the thought of receiving the treasured grade twelve diploma, and also as the planner of the event. Because I worked for the continuing education department promoting the program while also a student, I decorated for the ceremony and arranged for the newspaper reporter as well. Ours was the first graduating adult class in the county. Long hours of hard work and months of balancing school, work, and home life had paid off.

When an adult takes the plunge to go back to day school, you know the family has given up some everyday comforts to allow it to happen. There may have been times dust bunnies rolled under the living room sofa, or the family didn't get desserts as often, or a child had to share the kitchen table with Mom for schoolwork, as my daughter did. That same year, Melody graduated from grade eight, and many times we shared the kitchen table, each doing our homework. They say that children "catch" more than what you preach to them. Perhaps it was seeing me go back to school that motivated Melody to go to university when her turn came. She became the first in our family to do so. I was very proud of her. Many in our group had similar stories.

Our families had all lived through the struggle with us to be at this graduation. I think there should be a GMTS (Getting Mom Through School) award for the families of graduates. I knew that each family present could tell a story about the past year.

Family and friends gathered in the large meeting room set up for the graduation ceremony. But these were not ordinary family and friends. Instead of mothers and fathers coming to see their children graduate, the guests were the graduates' husbands, wives, and children. They were clearly proud of their graduates. Big smiles radiated from individual faces in the crowd. Gifts of flowers were tucked under chairs or held in little hands of children, ready to present to their graduate. Cameras were ready for the moment. Sitting in the front row with flowers clutched in hands, my husband and youngest daughter were both there to celebrate with me.

I had photographed the various classes and created a slide presentation with synced music, which played automatically while the students came into the room. Music to go with the photos had to be just right. Food and flowers for the reception had been ordered. Everything was perfect, and I was relieved!

During his remarks, Don Baker, my employer and our director of continuing education, quoted Dr. Anthony Campolo, a noted professor of sociology at Eastern College in Pennsylvania:

> *What you commit yourself to be, will change what you are and make you into a completely different person. Not the past, but the future, conditions you, because what you commit yourself to become,*

*determines what you are... more than anything that
ever happened to you yesterday or the day before.*

Today, I would love to meet Don Baker again and tell him that I kept his speech all these years, and how that quote became reality in my life. Just a few years after graduation, I was about to go through a complete paradigm shift in my life, one which at this point I had no concept of but which I was conditioning myself for nonetheless.

Our graduating class of students had committed themselves to a process. We followed the thread of knowledge, and the process changed us. The process not only built our self-confidence, but it opened up new opportunities for better employment in the future—or for some, a jumping-off point for higher education. What we had learned most deeply perhaps was that it is never too late to go back to school. I felt very proud of my achievement to complete my grade twelve diploma.

After the graduation, my thirst for knowledge was still not quenched. That fall I continued to follow the thread of knowledge to night school at a local community college. The adventure continued!

Jugendstil

Eyes Opened

> *"But until a person can say deeply and honestly, 'I am what I am today because of the choices I made yesterday,' that person cannot say, "I choose otherwise."*

> ~Steven Covey

Achieving a grade twelve diploma had such an impact on my life. I wondered about teens in jail because of poor choices. Were they getting help and encouragement to improve their situation once they left jail? A year after graduation, while still working for the department of continuing education, I was asked to research what the local jail system was doing to help the incarcerated teens improve their education.

The glorious spring day was just right for a ride in the country, but the gnawing anxiety about my destination haunted me like a phantom. I slid into the car and started out on my quest. The rays of the sun streamed through the window, warming my winter-weary soul as if to tempt me to a faraway beach. The twenty-minute car ride seemed to fly by. I tried to sort out the avalanche of thoughts that cascaded through my mind. What would it be like going into a jail? I was nervous and curious all at the same time. Before I knew it, I was pulling into the grounds of the correctional institution, more commonly known as the jail. My destination.

I was scheduled to talk to the principal about their continuing education program for inmates, students striving to get their grade twelve diplomas. Most of these students were still teenagers who had gotten in trouble with the law.

Driving down the long, winding driveway, I saw my first clue that this was not the office building it first appeared to be. Signs at strategic spots along my entry stated, "All cars *must* be locked on these grounds." Stopping my car in the parking area, a glance to the roof of the building gave me my second clue to affirm just where I was. In great cylinders along the top of the open areas were rolls of barbed wire, silent sentinels keeping watch over their charges.

The reception area could have been in any office building in any city. Men in white shirts with grey trousers and sweaters lounged against the reception desk. They looked like any office workers. After giving my name to the receptionist and sitting down to wait for the principal's secretary, my mind again started running wild. Observing the men lounging in the reception area, I wondered which one was the inmate and which was the guard.

Soon the secretary came to guide me to the principal's office. It seemed like a normal courtesy. However, I was soon to realize that a guest went nowhere in this building without an escort. I signed in with the name of my company and the person I was visiting and was given a number to pin on my lapel.

The secretary chatted on with small talk, slipping in a seemingly casual comment. "Oh yes, if you notice this tag missing, be sure to let someone know immediately, but not an inmate. They would love to get one of these tags!"

I sensed this was not as casual a statement as she tried to make it sound, and my nervousness racked up a little. My hands were sweating and I had butterflies in my stomach.

We stood in front of a large, electronically-controlled door. From somewhere inside the mirror-windowed cage, a button was pushed. The immense door slid open with amazing ease. As the secretary chatted on, obviously to abate any uneasiness I may have felt, we stepped through the door.

The door clanged shut behind us and we were in a cubicle, much like an air-lock chamber. Gradually, the second electronic door opened, and I found myself in a long hallway, like that of a hospital. I was surprised to see female guards passing as we proceeded down to the second air-lock type chamber. This led into the school area for the young offenders. Lining the halls of the office area were pieces of furniture. There were beautifully crafted coffee tables, bookshelves, and even a dresser, making it look like a furniture store. This puzzled me! The secretary explained that these pieces were made by the inmates and proudly on display here.

After my interview with the principal, the counsellor took me on a tour of the school. The thought struck me as we walked around that, except for the absence of girls, this looked just like my local high school. The boys were all under eighteen years of age. The school had different types of shops, as well as math, English, and basic literacy programs. Half a dozen boys were lounging in the resource centre or working on one of the three computers. It made me ponder. They looked like teenagers in any school library. I was never told what their crimes were, but I thought how sad it was that these young men were already labelled and their freedom taken away because of what I guessed had been foolish choices.

As we went through the woodworking shop, my guide stopped to introduce me to one of the boys working on a table. Mark had come into the institution's school three months previously—a rebellious, angry young man. After his assessment, Mark was put into a basic literacy program. It was discovered by one of the teachers that he was a learning-disabled person, just as I had been in school. After many long hours of counselling and nurturing, Mark asked the same teacher one day, "Do you really think I can learn to read?" Today he smiled at me as he sang the praises of his teachers by announcing, "I can even read 'cinnamon buns' on the label now." From my own recent experiences in school, I understood his excitement.

This was one clue as to why some of the boys were here and how helping them get an education could change their lives. Mark's progress was obviously the work of another caring teacher, like Marilyn, Jean, and Pat had been for me. Change one thing, and you can change everything! Education seemed to be the key to turn this boy's life around. I suppose when I arrived, I expected to see the TV scenario of people in caged cells, not this atmosphere looking like any high school in the county.

I was taken back to the principal's office and offered coffee while I waited for someone to escort me back to the front office. As I sat chatting with the principal about how the school was run, plying him with questions, it would be easy to forget I was in a jail. I was quickly brought back to reality when the phone jangled and the principal excused himself. "Two missing," he said sheepishly.

Shortly after, I was escorted to the front office and went through the same process as on entry, only in reverse. As we entered the last air-lock type chamber, my lapel number had to be put in a little sliding drawer, which went through to the guard in the mirror-windowed cage. All this had to be done before he would open the last electronic door to the lobby and grant me freedom to the outside world.

I slid back into my car again quickly and locked the doors behind me. Seeing barbed wire on the top of the building gave me a spooky feeling! It must be awful to be so close yet so far from freedom with a roll of razor wire separating you from the world. The sun again streamed through the car window, warming my winter-weary soul. I'd never been a winter lover and often day-dreamed my way through it about faraway beaches and summer vacation. Not this time.

Now as I drove out the curving drive, I noticed the renewing of life in the spring grass and the flowers bursting to announce their presence. How seldom I stopped in my busy schedule to enjoy a glorious spring day and to realize what a precious trea-sure freedom is. The students I met were still striving to get that grade twelve diploma and better themselves. Here I found echoes of my own life—caring teachers motivating students to reach and stretch to the sky and beyond to better themselves, even in a place of incarceration. It made me more determined to encourage young people to recognize how important it is to get a good education, and to be grateful for the education I was getting now. I knew how it felt in my own life to miss out on getting my grade twelve diploma as a teen, and how much more work it was achieving it at forty-three. I didn't have encouraging teachers when I was a teen, but the encouragement of the teach-ers I met as an adult changed my life. I hoped the same could happen now for the boys I met on this visit.

Following the Elusive Thread

Overcoming Fear

Therefore, since we are surrounded by such a great cloud of witnesses, let us throw off everything that hinders and ... let us run with perseverance the race marked out for us.

~ *Hebrews 12:1*

It was September 1987, still working for Halton Board of Continuing Education; I had decided to go to night school at Sheridan College to learn more. I was hooked now.

On my first night, students with briefcases swinging at their sides hurried down the hallway and disappeared. Long halls skirted around a glassed entrance area and then shot off in different directions. Not daring to hesitate too long, lest someone think I was lost, I followed the hallway, hoping for a sign to give me directions. A road map for this building would have been most helpful at this time. Terror! It hung over my head like a frozen block of ice as I stood there in the hallway. I had driven from Burlington to Oakville the previous day and found the college, the parking lot, and even the front door, but I had failed to find the classroom.

My new Levi jeans and Reebok runners were my feeble attempt to fit in as much as possible on the first evening. Panic ebbed and flowed like the river of students around me. They all appeared to have a predetermined destination, while I was confused by the labyrinth of halls. I wondered if I would ever find the right room. Perhaps it was a mistake to even entertain the dream of going back to school at my age.

I was carried along in the crush of students until ahead of me I saw the friendly face of a security guard giving directions. At last, the infantry had arrived to rescue me! After he pointed me in the right direction, I again followed the hallway until I found room E117.

As I stood at the door, dread enveloped me again. I felt like vomiting. Just as I was trying to decide whether to enter the room or bolt for the exit, a woman about my age came toward me. She looked intently at me, and I was afraid that she could see the terror in my eyes. Stopping directly in front of me, she asked, "Is this English One O One?" Chuckling to myself at the realization that I was not alone in my apprehension, I nodded, and we went into the classroom together.

Sliding into a seat on the far side of the room so that I could observe all the proceedings, I hoped that no one would notice me—particularly the teacher! I was relieved to see other mature students in the class. Perhaps I'd make it through the evening after all.

At forty-four, most of my female peers were settling down to think of grandchildren, and here I was just starting on my post-secondary education. I pinched myself to make sure that this wasn't just a dream. I had finally made it to college! But, of course, it was a dream—my dream for the future. Two years earlier I had begun my quest, and now I stood on the threshold of another door that I must open.

Fear continued to hound me, but I wouldn't quit. I'd been bitten by the learning bug. Each time I had to push through the fear to do something, I'd remember each of the new experiences I'd moved through successfully. I remembered how going to that first night school accounting course and getting a 95 per cent had started this journey. I had never achieved high marks like that at any point when I was going to school. My teachers from my teens would have been shocked! This gave me courage to push through the fear again and again, to grasp the prize on the other side of the doorway. The initial terror had passed, the process had begun, and the dream was becoming reality.

Facing the Dragons

"Change can be difficult, but it becomes easier when you do a little at a time."

~ *John Maxwell*

After that first night of college, I completed many classes, but the process was not going fast enough to quench my thirst for learning. It would take me forever to complete a college diploma at the rate of one course a semester! I decided to muster up all my courage! In 1989, after working for Continuing Education for three years, I quit my full-time job to go back to school full-time for a three-year Graphic Arts Production Coordinator college diploma.

At home, my youngest daughter was now in high school, and we still did our homework together at the kitchen table. Ralph was again supportive of my launching into this challenge, as he could see that it was improving my self-confidence. Neither of us realized the breathing dragon of change that was about to happen in our lives as I went through a real paradigm shift in my life. At first the difference between school and home life was minimal, but gradually as I progressed and changed, cracks formed in the marriage over the next three years.

In the summer of 1989, the week before school started in September, I called Gail in the registrar's office and asked her what happened on the first day of school.

"Just come on the first day and we'll have orientation," she replied. She sounded cheerful and full of confidence, but I was feeling very unsure of myself.

"No, no, you don't understand!" I pleaded. "What exactly do I do when I come through the front door? Where do I go?" After my first night of night school, I was determined to be prepared this time.

There was a long, pregnant pause, and then a bubbly little voice came over the telephone line with, "Find a corner, like I will, and hide in it!"

We both laughed. It was all I needed to get things back into perspective. She was right; I did survive orientation day.

I not only survived orientation day, but that first year of college flew by. Over the year I observed that Gail always had an encouraging word for students as she passed them in the halls. She was never too busy for a cheerful, "Hi, how are you doing?" Gail's comments always made me feel that there was someone out there that cared how I was coping in this new adventure.

During those first few months of college, there were many times I would walk down the halls muttering to myself, "What are you doing here? You must be crazy!" Sometimes it was only my dogged determination never to quit something once I started that kept me going. Never say die!

This determination to succeed had only grown in me over the last few years since I'd first gone back to school, so I didn't always feel it. Some days I'd be full of confidence, and at other times I'd be so discouraged, I was ready to pack it all in. Having poor self-image for so many years meant that it was a constant internal battle to overcome it. Still, there was always something that pulled me out of the funk.

There were times during college when I drove my instructors mad with my unending questions. Now that my mind had been unlocked from all those old expectations of my ability, it would race on. I would ask a question, and one particular teacher would say to me, "I haven't got there yet." It was like trying to control a runaway locomotive or fill a bottomless well. I had to stop myself from asking questions, but my mind kept saying, *Give me more ... more ... more!*

One day when passing through the front office, a voice called out to me. "Congratulations!" the chairman's secretary exclaimed to me as I was passing by her desk.

Confused by this unexpected honour, I blurted out, "Congratulations on what?"

"You don't know, do you?" she said. "You're on the dean's honours list, and it's going up today."

My father's saying, "Too soon old and too late smart" came to mind at this moment. But was it too late for me?

Five years earlier, I had a grade ten education, with a high school transcript showing that I had been a less than average student. When I was sixteen and in high school, there was no knowledge of learning disabilities; you were either smart or not. I never made it into the "dummy" class, but I struggled. I'd been a poor speller and had points taken off for it in every subject. To hear now that I was an honours student was almost more than I could take in. It had been a difficult decision to quit my job and come back to school full-time for three years at college, a decision that at times I questioned. Where would all this lead? I followed that elusive thread of knowledge, because I had decided to live life on purpose. There could be no turning back! It became my belief that it is never too late to seek, to find, to explore, or to discover.

Judith had an open-door policy as secretary of the counselling office at this campus of Mohawk College, and many students would feel free to just pop in to decompress. She was a great encourager! During the first few weeks I would pop in to see Judith, just to talk to someone over twenty-five. She was always cheerful and understood what it was like to come back to school as a mature student, as she had also upgraded her skills as a mature student. "Those first few weeks," she told me, "were the worst time of my life." She encouraged me to just keep going. Her whimsical attitude on life was infectious; you could not go out of her office feeling depressed. Halfway through the year, Judith got a new hairdo—permed, moussed, and sticking out in all directions. The students said she looked like a rock star now. Judith just laughed. Always ready to make fun of herself, she had a perspective on life that many struggle for. She was always a joy to be around, and the counselling office became a favourite place to go for a break.

These were the highs, but there were also the times when my old insecurities and inadequacies would haunt me like ghosts. The panic never totally leaves; I just learned to control it more effectively. Only one of my classmates knew of the times when the old panic would envelop and threaten to suffocate me. My new "buddy" was a Taiwanese student who was only twenty-two, but she had more maturity than many forty-year-olds. When I was down, she would be the one to encourage me with, "Just keep going, you can do it!" My family were big supporters and encouragers in my life at this time, but to hear encouragement from one of my school peers was special. She was going through the same process as I was!

One day fear reared its head again. Read my story in front of the business class? I was terrified! My early school experiences were negative, as I stumbled over words when reading and other students laughed at me. I tried to be as invisible as possible in class during those years so that I wasn't called on. That day I braced myself and walked hesitantly to the front of the room, knees knocking. I read my story and was surprised when the students didn't laugh. I heard them clap. Well, this was a new experience!

I had to get up and read several more times after that first oral reading exercise. I learned that I was becoming less nervous each time I got up to speak in front of people. The old saying, "There is nothing to fear except fear itself" was very applicable to me. I didn't like to be the centre of attention; however, I realized that I could hide my nervousness from people and just bluff my way through.

The better prepared I was, the less nervousness I felt. Even if I wasn't feeling well, I would bluff my way through again and hope for the best. Speaking in front of people became easier and easier with more practice.

I learned a great deal during that first year of college, and not all the learning came from books. The experience caused me to stretch and grow in my personal life. It caused me to question and evaluate how I reacted to circumstances around me, how I felt about issues, and what principles were worth the effort to stand up and be counted. Whereas before I had been afraid to let others know my thoughts on issues, or where I would have previously avoided an unpleasant confrontation, I was now learning appropriate ways to deal with issues and difficult situations.

My life at home and life at school were two different worlds. At school I was asked my opinion and often sought out for my opinion on issues, but at home I still got, "You don't know what you're talking about" when I started to express my ideas on issues. The cracks were starting to form in the marriage. How sad it made me feel to see things at home crumbling. I wanted us to be two strong individuals working beside each other instead of in two different worlds.

These life lessons weren't always easy, and sometimes they were downright painful, but they were part of the growing process and therefore essential. Expressing my own thoughts was particularly difficult for me because I had always qualified my input with someone else's statement on an issue.

Every action has a reaction. My reaction to life around me made me feel like a vibrant individual, and sometimes like a powerless victims of life's little episodes. I had lived in both camps, and this current life choice was by far the most exciting and fulfilling one ... living life "on purpose"! Even though I'd still meet the old perception of me in my personal life, I continued to tentatively express my opinion on issues, even on shaky legs.

Late Bloomer

When others bloomed
In garish profusion
Its gangly stock
Could not be seen
For the blazon colour
Of its peers

Yet now...
it dares
to be different

Blooming...
while others
lie dormant

Relishing...
in the
audacity
of it all

by: Trudy Bridle

While in college with a room full of students under twenty-five, I realized that I was really a late bloomer. I was reveling in the audacity of it. Today, many adult students are engaged in going back to school to upgrade their skill set.

THE TEST

___

My heart sank lower
As the teacher bent over
And laid down the dreaded test.
My knees felt like Jell-O,
But he said, "Be mellow,
It's only a test, don't you know?"

For two hours straight
I wrote and I wrote;
My wrist thought itself broke,
And my brain was squeezed
Out like a sponge.
But he said, "Be mellow,
It's only a test, don't you know?"

And finally finished,
My brain like cooked spinach,
I handed in that offensive test.
My knees felt like Jell-O,
But he said, "Be mellow,
It's only a test, don't you know?"

Now why do I fret
And my palms start to sweat
When they say it's worth
Thirty per cent of my mark?
Well the message is here,
I can't get it clear,

It's only a test, don't you know?

Stepping Stones

Success is gained in inches ... not miles. Once you find your why ...
you will be able to find your way. Why is your purpose. Way is the
path. When you find your why, your path automatically has purpose.

~ John Maxwell

Another familiar face... more clasping of hands ... more patting
on the back ... more excited conversation.

It was a warm, sunny day in September of 1990 as the students
at Mohawk College in Hamilton, Ontario gravitated to the picnic
tables on the patio outside the college doorways. Returning
students clustered in small groups. Glad to see my classmates
after a four-month break, I was enthusiastic to hear of others'
summer experiences. Our little group was animated as we tried
to cram as much as possible into the few minutes we had before
registration began.

Not wanting to cut our conversation short, we went as a
group to the allocated rooms to register at one minute to 11:00
a.m. The previous year we'd all sat in stony silence in the same
room while the instructor registered, photographed, and gave
out timetables to each of us. This year things had changed! The
air felt charged with our excitement at seeing one another again.

If any teacher had tried to control the class at this point, it would have been like trying to cap a gushing oil well. Fortunately, the teacher managing registration had the good sense to not even try. She got through the formalities as quickly and with as much humour as possible. There would be enough time to get down to work tomorrow.

As we came out of the room, I observed two first-year students. I could tell they were first-year students by the confused look on their faces. They hesitated in the middle of the hall, looking around as if they were lost in a big city. Understanding the look of panic, I hesitated before going off to my next destination and waited for the question I knew would come. "Where is the cafeteria?" one asked. I pointed them in the right direction, glad to help and feeling compassion for their experience. Chuckling to myself, I remembered my own apprehension the previous year when I stood outside the same door asking, "Where is the cafeteria?"

My second year of entry into college life was very different from my first. Now I knew the process and where classes were. There was more learning for me this year, more stretching, more discoveries. I had more confidence this year as I learned to use my voice and was starting to explore how I wanted to use it. It was an exciting potential of discovering the new me in this context. This was the beginning of the paradigm shift without me realizing it.

Later in the year, I attended an awards dinner at the college with my husband and two of my instructors. I had won the Mohawk College Short Story Contest that year with my story titled "Overcoming Fear." It was about my first night at college night school. I was very excited and trying to look cool, but my stomach was in knots. They asked me if I wanted to read my story or have someone else read it at the dinner. I chose to have someone else read it because of my fear to get up in front of people.

Having my work read to an audience, even if I wasn't reading it, was a huge accomplishment for me! When I say that up to forty years of age, I thought I was a dummy, that isn't a statement of false humility, but a statement of fact. I remember a time in grade nine French class when I tried to skip out of the final exam. Grade nine French was a compulsory lecture class, and because of my learning disability, I just didn't get it. The principal called my mother and said that I just needed to come and at least be there for the exam. So, at fourteen years old, I proceeded to sit there and write out all the questions in longhand and hand it in. I was surprised to get a 50 per cent as my final mark.

Over the three years of college life as an adult, I finally realized I did have a brain and an opinion that others valued. But it was a slow process! The seed that Jean Baker had planted when I was forty-two and in night school was starting to grow. When she asked me if I'd considered a career in writing, I remember laughing at her comment. She then told me that having a learning disability was not a measure of my intelligence. That statement changed my perspective, and I became addicted to learning. It was a major paradigm shift.

Now here I was in my second year of post-secondary education at forty-seven, winning an award for my writing. One more stepping stone on my journey! The staff took a picture of me receiving my award, and my story was published in the Mohawk College monthly newsletter and the yearly magazine.

I learned that poor self-image can stunt what you can accomplish in life, but sincere appreciation and encouragement can liberate you to achieve goals you never considered possible. Eventually I'd learn that even writing a book was achievable, one inch at a time. This liberation was changing my life.

The second and third year flew by and, before I knew it, I was at the end of the three-year college program. It had been a stimulating journey. I learned skills, expanded my sense of what I could do, developed self-confidence, and met new friends. I was a different person from the hesitant, fearful one who called to ask where to go when I came through the front door on registration day. Here I was at graduation day!

April 1992, Brantford, Ontario. I was forty-nine years old and sitting with my classmates in an auditorium packed with family and friends who had come to see us receive our diplomas. What a day! Three long years of hard work and stretching beyond our comfort zone had paid off.

I had worked with these students and they had become friends over the three years. I looked around and smiled. Elaine was a petite blonde, full of energy, and we used to joke in film stripping class that we were now "strippers." Now I chuckled, remembering that running joke we had for a while. Then there was Abby, my wise young Taiwanese friend, and many others. I had been called the "visible minority" during those three years, because I was the oldest student in the class. The rest of my class were in their twenties, but we worked as a team on the printing press or class projects. Age was no barrier to our connection. I had been accepted into the group even though I was old enough to be their mother. Strangers when we started, we now stood as friends on the threshold of a new adventure.

Our learning process had expanded my capacity in many ways as I learned how to think and express myself. I believe that's what college and university are really all about. It's not so much what you have learned, but how the process has expanded the capacity of your mind to consider new possibilities and other viewpoints.

This was just a theory of mine until I later read Dr. Oz and Dr. Roizen's book, *YOU: Staying Young* two years after graduation.

They wrote that the brain is an amazing muscle that can actually restore the power lines and regrow those neural connections. I remembered the old saying, "If you don't use it, you'll lose it." Apparently, research has proven this to be true about the brain.

Oz and Roizen's book addresses two ways we can decrease the risk of developing memory-related problems. We can become lifelong learners, and we can teach others. Research has shown that sharing your knowledge helps you retain information, and challenges your mind to learn. New ideas help regrow the neural connections in the brain, and that keeps your mind young and alert. Humans are living longer, and I personally want to get to old age with as many of my faculties in place as possible. Now at seventy-five, it doesn't sound like much fun being a hundred and not knowing what's going on around me. One of my heros where I now live in a seniors' complex is ninety-seven and still going downtown on the bus herself to the IMAX theatre. Amazing; she is inspirational!

I remember three months before I could attend college, I had to pass grade twelve math exams. I sat in a cubicle with head-phones and a book in front of a TV, learning each math topic for eight hours at a stretch to meet the deadline. I was never a math whiz. Since I'd been home raising my family for the past twelve years, it was difficult to learn the material and pass the exams. I would never forget going home from those intense cramming sessions. The left side of my brain would actually hurt at the end of the day. After reading about the brain's ability to regrow the neural connections, it makes sense that my brain hurt after these sessions. What an amazing body we've been given!

Now my well-exercised brain and I were at another graduation ceremony. This one was different from my grade twelve graduation with the adult learners program. We wore black gowns and caps as all college and universities wear, sitting anxiously in the front rows of the Brantford auditorium. Professors, garbed in official robes, sat in a row on the stage. I had made it! Waiting with great anticipation, I watched as one by one our names were called to come to the stage and receive the coveted diploma. Flashbulbs crackled and popped here also. But these were mostly mothers and fathers of the graduates, with a sprinkling of husbands and children. Ralph and Melody where here again with my two school-teacher neighbours as my rooting section. The pride of accomplishment was still there. One stepping stone had led to another, and another; I had survived. Each stepping stone had brought me to this day. I didn't know the future before me, but the process had changed me.

The adventure continues!

This photo, called "Reaching for the Sky," is by my friend Mona Lucas (Mona Lucas Photography on Facebook). It reminds me of the difficulty of overcoming to reach this amazing place in my life. There were many boulders on the way, but the light and little tree at the top represent the hope of the future.

Finding Hope in the Ashes

"For I know the plans I have for you," declares the LORD,
*"plans to prosper you and not to harm you, plans to give you
hope and a future."*

~ *Jeremiah 29:11*

I was a late bloomer, and now you couldn't stop me from flowering. Little did I know that the process of going back to school would create a paradigm shift and change me into a completely different person. Before going to school, I had been a dependent person with a poor self-image and no self-confidence. I'd never even consider expressing an original thought of my own. Oh, I had my own thoughts, but afraid of criticism and scorn, I would never express them. By the time I graduated from college, I realized I did have a brain, I was confident in my ideas and analysis, and I had a new sense of self-worth.

It was 1992 and I was forty-nine years old. After six years of hard work, I had achieved my academic dream of a post-secondary diploma and a career. During those six years of schooling, my husband Ralph had been my strong encourager and supporter in what I was doing. He cooked dinners and helped clean the house so I could study. I never could have achieved what I did without his support. We also had dreams as a couple of travelling around North America in retirement, enjoying our grandchildren, and possibly starting our own business. My future looked bright, but there were also some dark clouds on the horizon.

At this time, I was diagnosed with fibromyalgia and was learning how to cope with it. When it would flare up, I'd feel like a truck had run over me. Fibromyalgia feels like you've the aching body that goes with the flu, all the time. I'd been raised by three stoic women with rheumatoid arthritis who never complained. They just got on with life. So that's how I attacked this new diagnosis. I chose to have the outlook of my glass being half full, not half empty. For many years I was able to hide it and just sleep all day Saturday to cope with the next week. My close friends knew not to call me on Saturday. I had limited energy, so I had to be sensible in how I used it.

The three years after my graduation were a mix of excelling in my new career and extreme pain on the home front. My youngest daughter went away to university in the US. There was pain in seeing Melody leave home, but joy to see her expand her horizons, just as I had. After graduation, I'd also acquired an excellent job in a national office doing work I loved as a desktop publisher and administrative assistant. At work people respected my skills and thoughts, but at home, my marriage was in trouble. Here the pain was in the conflict of me becoming more independent and vocal, and my husband becoming withdrawn, quiet, and saying less than he ever had. Seeing my marriage to the love of my life crumble at my feet was painful. We went to counsellors and had long talks to try to salvage our marriage, but it was as though we were talking two different languages. After twenty-one years together, I pondered the failure of our marriage. And I don't like failure.

I realized that when one individual in a marriage goes through a catastrophic change of personality, both partners have to be on the same page with the changes that are happening, even if the changes are positive. The one changing is not the person the partner fell in love with and married those many years ago. When a person goes from dependency to independence, from poor self-image to confidence, the other person has to be okay with that change, or the marriage is in trouble. Also, communication is key. Unfortunately, communication had been the major challenge in our marriage. Ralph was not a man to share his feelings, and I was now asking him to do just that. I can only guess that it was frustrating to him. I thought fixing me would fix the marriage, but it had just driven a deeper wedge into the relationship.

At the time, I felt that every divorce was a failure in marriage, a reflection of a throwaway society I didn't want to participate in. Electronics were only made to last a certain number of years, and some people seemed to think the same of marriage. If it's too hard, too difficult, just move along to the next version. On top of all of this, the example of my parents' forever marriage was a strong impression in my psyche as the way I should be in relationship. When I was young, I was naive enough to buy into the TV sitcom idea that everyone got married and lived happily ever after. Where was my happily ever after?

In 1995 we divorced, and my dreams lay at my feet like the sandcastle I'd built as a little girl ... the one the storm came in and smashed. A sandcastle can be rebuilt, but what about a life or a marriage? I liked the confident, God-fearing person I'd become. Never could I go back to the dependent, insecure person I was before, but the divorce was a sad part of my life.

I grieved for all I had lost in life. All my lost dreams of the future had crumbled into lost love, lost family connectedness— the little and big examples of this. I loved our Christmas traditions, and they were smashed in the process of divorce. I had loved the gathering of family at Christmas, the special food, the sense of community, fun, and laughter. Now they were gone! And more than just this one time of year, I was so sad to lose the love of my life, my husband.

The divorce led to depression, which eventually was diagnosed as a clinical depression. On disability for six months because of the depression, I was shocked after having been free of it for so long. But here I was again. I lost my job because of not being able to cope when the wet blanket of exhaustion overwhelmed me. It felt like I was in a dark tunnel and there was no light at the end of it. But the advantage I had this time was that I knew the symptoms and knew I had to do something positive to pull out of it. Finally, I realized I had a choice: wallow in self-pity, or build new dreams. I went to a workshop on recovering from depression, and one exercise changed my outlook and led me to healing. I put together a collage of pictures of things and people that were still in my life. I had lost so much, but it made me realize what I still had. It hung on my wall for many years. I still have it. As I picked up each picture that became a piece of the collage, I picked up the positive aspects of my current life. I had my children, extended family, love of travel, love of music, good career, and a desire to continue to grow. I decided to focus on what I did have and build new dreams. Sad about what I had lost, I liked the person I had become! I reframed my world.

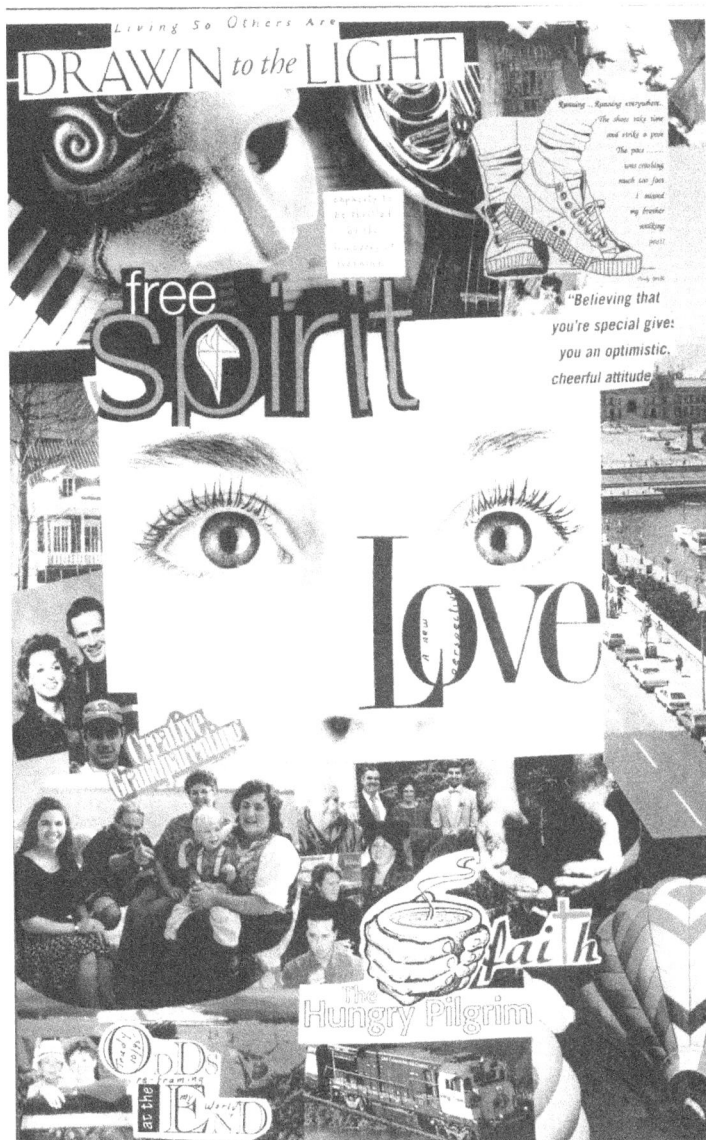

This is the first collage I did after a clinical depression,
and it made me realize all I did have in my life.

The time of recovery gave me the opportunity to analyze life and determine the true meaning of success. How do you measure true success in life? Is it having lots of money, or a big house, beautiful furniture, a flashy car, vacations in the Bahamas? Is that truly success?

Pondering that very question made me realize that success isn't about money or possessions. While those things are nice to have, they're not permanent. I couldn't take them with me, and they would fade away. I could lose them in a flash! People won't remember how much money I made or the house I lived in. They will remember how I made them feel.

I wanted to leave this earth a little better than when I came into it. I wanted to pull that one burning dream from deep within myself and make it happen. I wanted to share my knowledge with others on the journey, no matter how painful it was, helping others recognize and achieve their own dreams.

John Maxwell says in his book "*Intentional Living, Choosing a Life that Matters*", "To be significant, all you have to do is make a difference with others wherever you are, with whatever you have, day by day."

I decided to live a solo life. I carried on developing new dreams, travelling much over the years, and working in areas of the country I'd always wanted to live in. Life was an adventure I chose to live intentionally. My children were all married and on their own, so I created a new life. I was committed to guarding my integrity and acting with honour in my dealings with people. Reframing my world began.

After recovering from the depression, I remembered my long-ago dream of working in British Columbia. When I'd still been in nursing school and living in the YWCA, I had a desire to travel and dreamed of going to work in BC after reading about it.

Now in 1996, I gathered all the courage I could and called Andrea, an old acquaintance that had moved to Victoria. Asking if I could room with her while I looked for a job, I was thrilled when she said yes. We've had many jokes about that phone call since. Apparently, she couldn't place me when I called, and it wasn't until she had spoken to a mutual friend that she remembered and agreed to have me come and live with her family. Andrea is the person I lived with for six months when I came to BC in 1996.

I got on a plane, unsure of where I would be staying or if I would find a job, but I had to try. My knees knocked with fear during that period. For the two years I lived in BC, I healed and put my life together again. Every day I would go out to the Victoria library and look for a job. It was terrifying, but I wouldn't give up!

In 1996 when I was looking for a job there, two ladies prayed for me and gave me this verse that became my life verse to this day. Jeremiah 29:11: "'For I know the plans I have for you,' declares the Lord, '"plans to prosper you and not to harm you, plans to give you hope and a future."'" I have found it to be true over the years.

People in BC had no preconceived idea of how I *should* act, so they accepted me just the way I was. *Should* is such a nasty word, and there in BC I released it. I was able to pick up the pieces of my life that I liked and disregard the negative aspects that I didn't like. Speaking my own thoughts was accepted as normal, and there was no one who told me, "You don't know what you're talking about." It was liberating! I discovered that life was an adventure if you have the courage to step out of your comfort zone, even when fear has you trembling. Tenacity was essential, and it wasn't always easy.

Looking back in a journal from that time, I found a quote one day that I only had 91¢ left. It was not long after that I got a call for an interview at a copy shop in Sidney. It had taken six months to find a job, and Andrea and her family became fast friends that I now call my BC family.

The following years were filled with the blessings of travel, new work, and starting a business at sixty years old. I had found hope. I was like a phoenix rising from the ashes of my previous life to embrace this new life. And it was a good life! I liked the person I had become, through the ashes of failure, and through the life of adventure I chose to live intentionally with integrity and hope. Life is precious, so I would use it now to encourage others on their journey.

Reframing my World

When you intentionally use your everyday life to bring about positive change in the lives of others, you begin to live a life that matters.

~ *John Maxwell*

For two years I worked as a desktop publisher in the printing industry in Sidney, on Vancouver Island, BC. When I was laid off during a recession, back to Ontario I went to get more computer training. During the six-month business school program, I became a Microsoft Office User Specialist, giving me the ability to teach software. Sometimes I thought about the skill set I'd gained as a nurse but figured it was something I'd probably never use again. I couldn't see how my nursing background and my current software training would ever morph into one job. They seemed to be at opposite ends of the spectrum. But God knew what He had planned for me! In a year, I would see the marrying together of those two skill sets.

After finishing my computer training in the winter of 1999, before looking for another job, I embarked on a three-month trip across Canada on a Greyhound bus. Living life intentionally became my theme. Stopping at bed and breakfast accommodations across Canada, I would ask the locals what I needed to see. Then off I would go, either walking or on the local bus, to explore the city. It was an amazing time! Travelling solo was a wonderful experience. I discovered that when you travel alone, other people are more apt to talk to you than when you travel in a pair. Seeing the breadth of Canada is a great experience, one I believe all Canadians should have once in their lives.

When I returned to Ontario, I needed a job. The province was going through health care reform, and I was fortunate enough to get a job in Dr. Copps' office. My earlier skills as a nursing assistant and my current computer skills were finally married together in a job helping a doctor's office become computerized. That job led to a position at a medical clinic in McMaster University, helping with the same issue. I'd grown up in a society of twenty-five-year jobs, but that was not the current job market.

After a year working at Dr. Copps' office, with my contract completed, I began to think of going out West again and had an air ticket and a mover booked to move out to BC. I had fallen in love with Vancouver Island, and the pull was to go back there. Then I heard of a doctor at McMaster University who also needed help with health care reform. If I wanted to advance my career in the job market of that time, I had to learn to move laterally to other companies that produced advancement in my area of expertise.

It was quite funny how I approached this job. Considering my earlier job-hunting experiences, it was quite arrogant of me. Never in my job-hunting career had I ever considered being in control of the interview like this regarding my future working conditions. It was part of the new me. When David offered me a job to pull the Ontario Health Insurance Plan billing away from a third-party biller, I hesitated. Finally, I offered to come and work for him for a month, in which time we would both get to know each other and see if I wanted to cancel my plans to move to BC. All it took was two weeks for me to catch David's passion. Another stepping stone that would change the direction of my life.

I was very fortunate to meet Dr. David Chan, who had a vision of creating software to digitalize doctors' offices. Dr. David Chan was a man with a dream in 2001! His passion was to develop leading-edge medical software to help doctors treat their patients more effectively. At this point, I reminisced about working in a bookstore in 1985 and then continuing to studying for a grade twelve diploma. It was hard to realize that I was now working at McMaster University in 2001.

Over the next two years, David became my boss, teacher, and eventual mentor. I pulled the provincial health care billing away from a third-party biller into the local clinic. In between patients, David would pop up to the space where I was working to see how I was doing on the billing and to express how impressed he was with what I was doing. It resonated deep in my soul to be affirmed by a man I greatly respected. He never knew what a huge leap from my past this was. Later, when I started a service provider business of his software, he became my mentor and encourager.

Before the new medical software system was in place, doctors would write the patient's diagnosis on a piece of paper and it would go to another building downtown for another person to process the billing. With the new system David created, the doctors entered their own billing at the point of entry, and I just submitted it to the government agency for payment. This eliminated many errors in trying to figure out the doctor's writing. The doctors loved having me right in the clinic to answer their billing questions. Dr. Chan changed an old DOS program he had created at McGill University so I could send the bills to our provincial Ministry of Health. But that was only a stopgap for

David. His real passion was to create free open source software that would run a doctor's office. It would include appointments, billing, and a new concept—electronic medical records. David called the open source software OSCAR.

Often David would say to me, "The gifted people of the world love to create new things and then just give them away." He was never interested in setting up a business. The fun to him was in the development of something new that would help doctors make better decisions with their patients.

I had the privilege of working with the first design team of the OSCAR medical software program. Eventually, I became the technical writer and trainer for the software as it launched in October of 2001. Here my skills from nursing, software training, and desktop publishing were truly married together. I finally experienced the plan of the God of the universe in my life. God's timing is perfect! The job was not ready for me in 1999 when I worked at the doctor's office learning provincial billing. Now, I had the skill set to accomplish the job before me.

In 2003, two years later, as funding was running out again, I thought it was time for me to retire at sixty years of age. I knew a couple of doctors in BC who wanted to use OSCAR, so out I moved. Developing and presenting a seminar to doctors, and visiting many doctors' offices to demonstrate OSCAR, resulted in five clinics around Vancouver adopting the OSCAR program to run their offices. This was the leading edge of software development, and I was the first person in Canada to set up a business as an OSCARservice provider. Money was tight, and I was living off my savings, because even when I got a new client it wasn't enough income to sustain a person. It was exhilarating and scary at the same time!

After two years in Vancouver, Dr. Chan asked me to go back to Ontario in 2005. Since there was no one in Ontario setting up an

OSCAR business, he asked if I'd come back to set up a business promoting the software. I handed my five BC clinics over to a local trainer to continue support and moved back to Ontario.

Growing the business was a challenge at times. The road to success needed some improvement along the way, and in 2006 I enrolled in a Dale Carnegie program at my office building. What a good decision! How to speak in front of a group and how to deal with difficult people were two of the valuable skills I learned.

I had one difficult client. Actually, that is an understatement. He used all of the three Cs I learned not to do in the Dale Carnegie program: complain, criticize, and condemn. Most of my clients were great to work with, but this one client was very stressful to deal with. In my past experience with difficult people in my life, I'd just avoid them. You can't do that when you're in business and dealing with a client. I was frustrated! I tried to accommodate his needs, even putting a staff person between us, but nothing seemed to work. The conflict between us was so distressing that I was at the point of considering firing him as a client.

Dale Carnegie gave me tools that turned the relationship completely around. One day I got a phone call from this problematic doctor. He wanted to talk to me because he felt one of his colleagues had wrongly represented him. For two hours I listened. I kept saying over and over to myself, *Don't criticize, condemn, or complain!* I thanked him for calling and expressing his perspective.

Before taking the course, I would have interrupted his rant to justify myself. This time, not until I had listened for one and a half hours did I insert how distressed I was about the fact that he was unhappy with our service. I told him that all our other clients were happy with our service, and he was the first to express dissatisfaction.

OSCARservice office with Toby Bian, my programmer.

Suddenly he was asking how he could help with other doctors. The conversation ended on a positive note, and we continued to have a great relationship. The tools I learned from Dale Carnegie made the difference!

I learned that when I really listened, I made the other person feel important. Difficult people who complain really want to feel important. His angry feelings dissolved, and he then worked to cooperate with the other doctors. This was what I really wanted. He became one the best promoters of the program.

Another Dale Carnegie skill I learned was encouragement and how it can change a person's life! This just reinforced the value of all of the motivation and encouragement I'd received on my journey of learning, and how it had helped me to become a lifelong learner.

One morning, Toby, my head programmer in the business, approached me with an idea. He thought our company should offer different bundles of services the way large organizations like Rogers and Bell do. His ideas were solid. Ideas had been buzzing around my mind for the past month, but I hadn't put them to paper. I stopped what I was doing and listened. Listening is another Dale Carnegie skill!

"That's great!" I said. "Why don't you write your thoughts down in an email and send it to me."

Later in the afternoon, Toby informed me that an email with his thoughts was on its way. I opened it and printed the attachment. That's when I was totally blown away. Toby had written out a complete two-page marketing plan to offer our services to clients in a new way. It was exactly what I had been looking for and more. He wasn't thinking of just himself, but of how the company could improve.

Did I value Toby more today than yesterday? You bet! The encouragement helped Toby to grow in confidence as well. He eventually purchased the business from me and grew it to three times its size during his first six years running it.

Encouragement tastes sweet ... like the filling of an Oreo cookie. Encouragement from one teacher changed my life. I wanted to pay it forward. I've always tried to encourage others, but since going to Dale Carnegie, I've been more intentional in encouraging people when I have the opportunity. I've been amazed at the results when sincere encouragement is dispensed. It's like watching a flower bloom as people see new possibilities in their lives.

One of my encouragers while I was in Dale Carnegie was Matt Pomeroy. He was young enough to be my son, but he motivated me to continue my writing. On Dale Carnegie graduation night, when I had to present my final talk, Matt introduced me with this statement: "This next person is the queen of reinventing herself. Changing everything from her locale, marital status, education, to her career, she has taken life by the horns and thrown herself in 110 per cent—not naively, but courageously. Of course, she has set new goals for herself, yet again. Judging by her great versatility and genuine concern for everyone, she will achieve these goals too. Please help me welcome up the ever-versatile trudy chiswell." This introduction was a shock to me! Sitting on the hard, plastic chair, my knees trembling, it was a few minutes before I could gather myself and get up to give my little speech. While a shock, the encouragement felt like a cold drink on a dry day. It isn't often that you know how other people perceive you. It was very encouraging.

By 2010, the Ontario business had grown to fifty-two clinics, supporting 180 doctors. I had three full-time salaried staff plus myself, and every day I was amazed at what I was doing. The seven years it took to build my business was an answer to prayer. Having fibromyalgia, it was getting more difficult to work a nine-to-five day-job. With my own business I was able to work and rest when I needed to. This allowed me to work seven years more than I would have been able to in a nine-to-five office setting. The business also provided for my retirement when I sold it in 2010, seven years after starting a business at sixty in BC.

What an amazing opportunity I had during those ten years! Catching the dream and passion of Dr. David Chan back in 2001, I was blessed to have been a part of seeing a dream become reality. Many new OSCARservice providers came on board during my last few years running the business. The Ontario business I began in 2005 had tripled by 2014 with the new management of my original programmer, Toby Bian. The OSCAR software that Dr. Chan dreamed of is now at the core of a thriving business and offers an affordable means for doctors to digitalize their office practices.

I suffered from unrecognized learning disabilities in school, received my high school diploma when I was forty-five and a college diploma at forty-nine, and started my own business at sixty. These circumstances, disabilities, and age had not held me back. My transformation happened because the mentors I had along my journey encouraged me to strike out and grasp the ring, and because I refused to give up! To bring about change in my life took tenacity, perseverance, and a dogged determination that I could do it. I took the first step toward my dream and then hung on no matter how long it took. What did it really matter how long it took? Life was an adventure, and I knew God had a map for me.

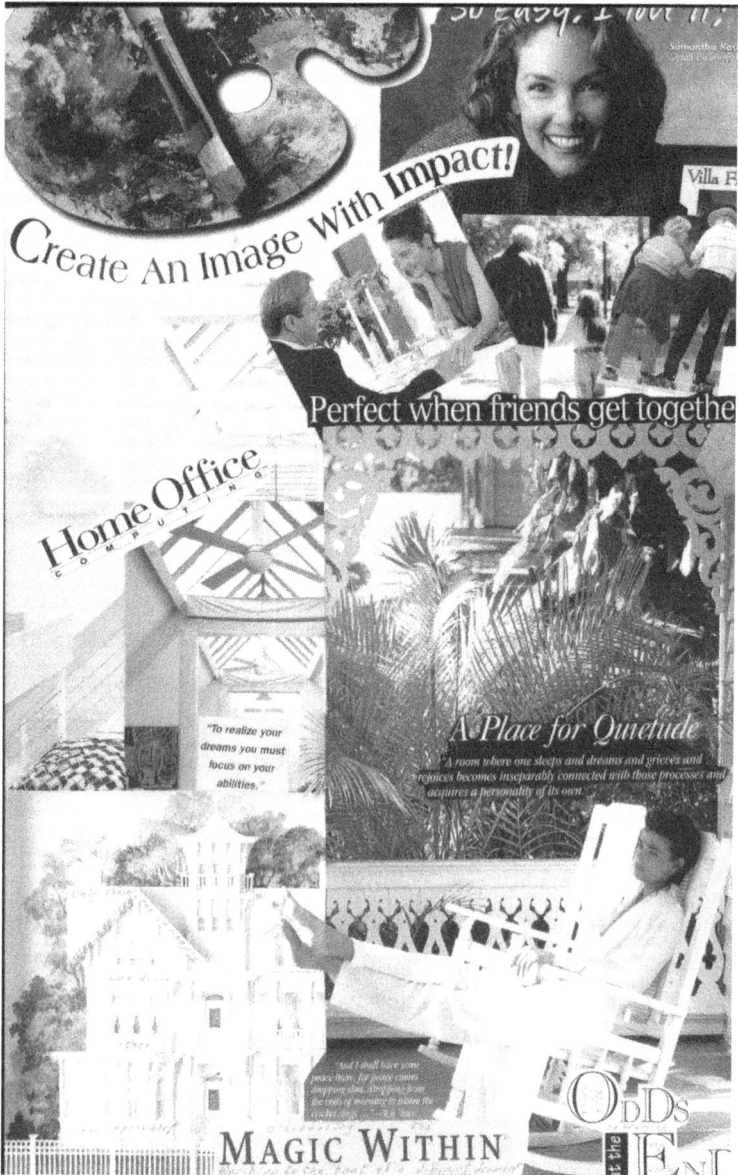

This is the second collage I did of my hopes and dreams to be an entrepreneur.

Finding Home

To Move ... or Not to Move?

He put a new song in my mouth, a hymn of praise to our God.

~ Psalm 40:3a,

My youngest daughter, Melody, had moved to Florida in 2005, and while running the business, I would go down to visit her family three or four times during the year. Every time I'd come into the airport the family was there to greet me with children jumping up and down with excitement that I was there. My son-in-law encouraged me to move closer! It was rewarding to be in a place where the family loved me and wanted me to be near them. Over the years of watching the grandchildren grow up, the thought of retiring in Florida became a passionate dream. How to do it?

I was now sixty-five and retirement age, but I couldn't just leave the business with the fifty doctors' offices we supported, but I was getting tired and the fibromyalgia worse. I spent months researching what would happen to my Ontario pension,

how to get US medical coverage, and the immigration require-
ments of the US. I hired an immigration lawyer to process the
papers with my Florida family sponsoring me to immigrate.
The dream of retirement to be near Melody's family and the
beach, and no more snow, was getting a little closer. I started the
process of trying to sell the business. Not an easy proposition!

It took a year of interviewing many different people who
were interested in the business, because I was the first one in
Canada and had the foundation of the client base. Eventually it
came down to who would be the best person to carry on and
understand our clients. In August of 2011, I sold the business
to Toby Biane, my programmer. My dream to sell everything in
Ontario and retire to Florida to be near my daughter Melody and
her family became a reality.

I sold most of my possessions on Kijiji, packed some memo-
rabilia and small items into a storage locker, and loaded my car
with everything I thought I needed until I got established. For six
months I lived with my daughter and her family while I looked
for a home I could afford. At first, I thought I would rent, but it
ended up being cheaper to purchase a small house. I was fortunate that Florida was at the bottom of a real estate recession.

I purchased a little two bedroom, two bath house for an
amazing $66K. The first time renovating and furnishing a house
with only my ideas of what should be done was another new
adventure. I loved it! My son-in-law was a big help to me, doing
some of the grunt work of tearing down to help me save money.
I researched three contractors for each segment: plumbing,
drywall, electrical, and kitchen cupboards. It was exhilarating
and so rewarding. The little house of my retirement dreams!

My son sent my storage locker possessions down with a
friend. I found a church that I enjoyed and made good friends,
who I still communicate with now. It hadn't been an impulsive

move. There had been three years of research and the hiring of an immigration lawyer before coming down. Another castle of dreams seemed to be complete.

I wasn't completely retired. I was still doing medical billing via the Internet for five of my previous business clients at OSCARservice. For two years I would sit with my desk in front of the window of my sweet little home, billing doctors who were in Canada, then take my grandchildren to swim in the pool in the afternoon. What a life! God had answered many prayers, and I was living my dream.

Two years after finishing renovating the house, I took a month to visit friends in Canada and California for my seventieth birthday, and now, finally, I had to face the issues of Florida health care costs. I discovered that all my previous research was incorrect. Because I was seventy and had not paid into the US Medicare system over a working lifetime, it wasn't available to me. I could buy into it for over $800 a month for basic health care coverage. This would not cover the 20 per cent that Medicare didn't pay or any medications. When I did my earlier research, this information wasn't available, and even my immigration lawyer had thought I'd be eligible for Medicare after two years. To say I was devastated was an understatement!

Why? I asked God. I thought this was to be my final move, my little retirement place. For two years I'd revelled in being close to my daughter and grandchildren and had made some amazing friends. Now, for six weeks I wallowed in confusion. Did I not hear God? Was it really on my own strength that I'd made this move? Had I jumped ahead of God's will in my life? Hard to say. Here I was in the US and finally coming to the conclusion that life down in Florida was not financially sustainable.

In December of 2013, after six weeks of confusion, I finally accepted the Lord nudging me and realized that it was time to go back to Canada. Finding a realtor, staging my home, and deciding what I would save or sell, I started the process. The realtor talked me into listing before I left for Canada, convincing me it took a long time to get the process going. I wasn't really in a hurry to sell. If it was the direction God wanted me to go in, it would sell; if it didn't sell, I'd stay another year. So I gave the realtor some strict parameters as to price and added that I didn't want to move until the end of April when it was warmer in Canada. I left it in God's hands and went off to Canada.

In December of 2013, I'd also gotten a call from a dear friend's daughter, saying that her mom, Vera, was dying and had asked for me. I spent an amazing six weeks with Vera in Ontario. She was a woman of real courage and strength who always shared the reason for her hope: Jesus! What a sweet soul Vera was. I would drive an hour from Burlington to Cambridge and we'd just sit and chat, catching up on each other's lives. She died six weeks later during a terrible snow storm, and I was privileged to give a eulogy at her funeral. It solidified to me how fragile life was. We worry about the material things in life, such as job, house, nice clothes, or how much money we have in the bank. All of that counts for nothing at the end of life. The important things are the relationships you make along the way. That's what people will remember.

During those six weeks, I experienced the worst winter weather Ontario has had since I was a child. And I remembered that I hate snow! After my house was on the market for five days, I received a call that it had an offer for six thousand more than it was listed at. Sold? Shocked! Amazed! The only snag was that the people wanted it a month before I wanted to move. I guess the Lord was sending me a message that coming back to Canada was the right move. But all that snow! Rationalizing that with an extra six thousand I could rent a condo on the beach until Canada got warmer in May, I accepted the offer.

Now what? Where to live, what to take, and what to sell? How do I do all this? A lot of people have dreams that are crushed and don't survive. It was my faith in the God of the universe and the confidence in knowing He had a plan for my life that allowed me to keep picking up my feet and moving forward each time these dreams lay smashed at my feet. I tend to see God in retrospect, and it wasn't until two years after this that I could fully see how I benefitted from living in Florida for those two and a half years. As a Christian, I didn't gauge how blessed I was by whether I was happy, or if things were going well. I trusted Him in the blind spots too, when He seemed to pull the rug out from under my feet and change the road map. I had wonderful times with the family and ended up making money on the house, which gave me security for a better retirement.

I decided to plan one month at a time and trust God to open the next door for me. Arranging an estate sale to sell all my possessions, and securing a condo on the beach for the month after the house sale, I had two months organized. Then the decision about how to travel back to Canada—drive my car, fly, or take a cruise through the Panama Canal and land in Vancouver, BC? Of course, my lust for travel picked the cruise through the Panama Canal. Landing in Vancouver after twenty days at sea, I went to stay with my dear friend, Andrea, for a visit. Before I left Florida, I said to Melody that perhaps I should explore retiring in Victoria. Her response was, "Why not? You've talked about nothing but BC since you went out there in 1996." I was open, but hesitant.

June 2014 in Victoria was wonderful. The outcome of my search for an apartment took an unexpected and surprising turn on my last planned day in Victoria. The scripture verse that had been given to me by those ladies in 1986 came back to mind. Jeremiah 29:11: "'For I know the plans I have for you,' says the Lord, 'plans to prosper you and not to harm you, plans to give you hope and a future.'" Now I also had a gift from a friend, a ring with the same words inscribed on it. Many times over the previous months I'd repeated that verse to myself as a reminder that God had a plan for my life, even at seventy. Living a solo life had been a challenge at times, but always I had that promise of God in my life. The power of this verse had been proved to me again and again over the years. As I explored the possibility of retiring in my favourite place in Canada, I experienced it again.

I prayed that God would show me in a dramatic way if this was the right move. It was a difficult decision, because my children were out East and in Florida. The big question was: Do I live in a place and climate where I don't thrive but to be near my children, or do I move to a place that speaks to my soul, where I have friends, and visit my children when possible? I didn't know at the time, but two years later, my granddaughter would choose the University of Victoria as the place to finish her education. It turned out that God did have a plan for my life and I would be seeing my children, even in Victoria.

I looked at many apartments in different locations—furnished suites, seniors' housing, and I even took a one-and-a-half-hour bus ride to check out co-housing. I wanted to keep my options open so that I could hear from God.

I had fallen in love with the James Bay area of Victoria. Short walks would get me to the ocean, to the grocery store and village centre, and to Victoria's Inner Harbour. I enjoyed trips to the ocean to sit on a bench and watch the sun go down, or I could hop a bus and go downtown to have Chinese food for supper. I just loved the area.

Finally, during the last week I'd planned to search for apartments in Victoria, with no big revelations from God, I decided that I would rent a furnished apartment for the winter and decide in the spring if this was really where I wanted to settle for the rest of my life. There are so many nice furnished apartments in Victoria because of tourism and the politicians coming and going to the government buildings. I decided furnished accommodation would be my best alternative for now. Well, God had other plans!

During this time, I'd also been checking out churches and seniors' centres. My first couple of weeks of church shopping had not been very successful. I have three criteria for a church home: good Bible teaching, good praise team music, and friendly people. I just didn't feel it with my first few experiences. In my third week, I went to a church where a jazz singer I knew of was featured in the service during Jazz Week in Victoria. I enjoyed the music, but it didn't feel like a good fit otherwise.

On the way back to the condo, I passed an old historic Anglican church that my friend mentioned was part of the new Anglican Network in Canada. They're a group of Anglican churches that feature a combination of Anglican liturgy with an evangelical focus. That particular Sunday there was a 4:00 p.m. service called "The Table." I decided to go. I found very friendly people, great music, and solid teaching of God's Word. There were lots of young people and children. After communion, I asked someone to pray for me about relocation. At the end of the prayer, the woman prayed that God would also surprise me. Well, He did just that the next week!

The following Sunday I went back to the morning service on Canada Day. Friendly people, great music, and good preaching! Check, check, and check! They invited me to the hall for tea and Canada Day cake. Sitting with the woman who brought me in to tea, I soon saw a couple enter the room and look around for a place to sit. Eventually they joined us, and I was introduced to Doris and Berk, retired professionals doing volunteer work in the Philippines. We got into a lively discussion about what they do in the mission field. I peppered them with question upon question and found their work inspiring. "What kind of work do you do there, what is the weather like, how did you find this position?" I asked. My curious mind again wanted to know more, more, more.

They also loved travel, as I did. It turned out that starting in August, their apartment would sit empty while they were in the Philippines for six months, so I asked them if they ever considered renting it while they were gone. I told them I was looking for a place to stay for the winter to decide if Victoria was the place to retire in.

Doris asked me back to their apartment for lunch, and we had such a great visit that it was 4:00 p.m. before I was heading back to my place. I felt like I had known them forever! They even had a stack of one of my favourite author's books that they were reading for the second time. And it turned out that their apartment was across the street from where I was staying.

The next day, on my last day in Victoria, I received an email from Berk saying that they would like to rent their apartment to me if I was still interested. There was that surprise from God! Doris and Berk's three-bedroom apartment is on the tenth floor, across the road from the ocean on Dallas Road. Oh yes, I liked heights as well! God says He will give us the desires of our heart. I hadn't even asked for this in my prayer about apartments, but God in His graciousness made it happen. Doris and Berk's apartment was a real gift. And so my adventure continued, and who knew where the story would lead? Oh yes ... God did!

My First Christmas in Victoria

"To reach a port we must sail, sometimes with the wind,
and sometimes against it. But we must not drift or lie at anchor."

~ Oliver Wendell Holmes

It was 2014, my first Christmas in Victoria. My first year away from family and friends, and I expected to be lonely. When January 3 arrived, I was pleasantly surprised to discover that I hadn't been lonely at all, and in fact had had a most enjoyable Christmas season. I had chosen to live life intentionally, so I approached Christmas that year with the same attitude. I chose to become an active participant in the city around me.

Victoria is a beautiful city, and no more beautiful than at Christmas, with all the sparkling lights. Coming home on the bus at the end of November, I noticed the parliament building lit up in the daytime. Strange! Later that night, my query was answered when I could see, from my balcony, the parliament buildings ablaze in coloured lights. Next day I noticed a big white tent in front of the Empress Hotel. Puzzled again! This turned out to be a new skating rink. Being from Ontario, where cold weather encourages skating rinks, this was not what I expected in Victoria with its winter flower gardens.

I served at a high tea and bake sale at my church, all lace, fancy sandwiches, and home baking. Great combination! I loved the acronym of my church: COOL, for **C**hurch **O**f **O**ur **L**ord. I still tell everyone I go to the COOL church! After being on my feet for a long afternoon of serving at the event, I thought I was too tired to go to the truck parade that same night. To my surprise, when searching online I discovered the truck parade went right past my apartment. You guessed it! I threw on my coat over my PJs, slipped into my shoes, bundled up in my hat and scarf, and went out to join the throng. Along with the children, I cheered the gaily decorated trucks beeping Jingle Bells as they streamed by the building. Pictures from my balcony on the tenth floor were unique and sent back to my truck-loving grandson in Florida.

Another Saturday afternoon I went downtown, intent on going to Market Square for the tuba concert. As I strolled down Government Street, I enjoyed the Christmas carollers on the corner, and I browsed the Pop-Up Market along the street on my way to Market Square. I wondered what this tuba concert would be like. It was wonderful to see Market Square packed all around the balcony, with Christmas music wafting up from the courtyard below. Eighty-five tuba players from across the island and lower mainland played as if they had been together for years. Amazing! After snapping many pictures and enjoying the music, I carried on with my stroll around town. At Bastion Square I saw the stop for the free horse-drawn trolley rides being offered by the downtown business association. I hopped on and thoroughly enjoyed a ride around town in the open trolley. I was fortunate enough to be on the last trolley ride of the day and got a ride all the way home as they went back to their trailer at Ogden Point, just down the street from my apartment. It was a lovely afternoon enjoying the city. I loved just wandering around the streets of Victoria and discovering my new home. I even started writing up walking trails for the local newspaper. I would meander down pathways, trails, and through parks around James Bay and then write about how much I enjoyed the community so that others could travel the same route. One article was about all the ice cream places I found in the area. I LOVE ice cream.

Two weeks before Christmas, my friend Andrea came over from the mainland to stay with me for five days. We became tourists in Victoria. Walking down to the Inner Harbour, we enjoyed the parliament buildings all dressed out in the finery of twinkling lights. More pictures! The lights were magical as we walked down Government Street past the skating rink and into the Empress Hotel. We strolled past the wonderful display of decorated trees from the different businesses of Victoria. The contest was in full swing for the best tree. What a lovely old building the Empress is! As we weren't in a hurry, we also enjoyed walking around the city as Christmas shoppers scurried around to find that perfect gift. Not having a list to fill, we could just enjoy the busyness of the holiday without being part of the craziness. A unique perspective! Starting this new life in the middle of life, while a challenge at times, was exhilarating! This was a time in my life when I was supposed to be set in my ways, but instead I was embracing new experiences and turning expectations upside down. Life was good.

Craigdarroch Castle at night looks rather spooky with the lights shining up the exterior. We went one night for a special tour of the castle and a viewing of the movie *Little Women*. Some of the scenes in the movie were filmed right there in the castle on Joan Crescent. The Historical Society had done a marvellous job restoring some of the rooms to period décor of the 1890s when the castle was originally built. The movie was shown in the ballroom on the fourth floor, and I couldn't help speculating how the ladies of that time climbed the four flights in their big hooped skirts. The view of Victoria from the widow's walk room was awesome.

Of course, it wouldn't be Christmas without a visit to Butchart Gardens at night to see the Christmas lights. The twelve days of Christmas were portrayed in lights throughout the garden. Joined by another friend, we had much fun singing the song as we came to each display. We even took a ride on the merry-go-round—at our age! You have to be a little silly sometimes in life. Dinner at the Gardens finished off the evening.

The next day it was back to the mainland on the ferry to spend the week before Christmas at my friend's daughter's home. With four children in the house, everything was about Christmas as the excited little people were all about family traditions. There was the children's Christmas pageant to see, visiting friends, and Christmas Eve midnight service. An extended family gathering on Christmas day for little gift exchanges, a big Christmas morning breakfast, and the Christmas dinner later meant we all had a wonderful day. The family keeps traditions that focus on the meaning of Christmas instead of the materialism that marketing tries to push on us. I was made a real part of this little family's Christmas, not just a guest. Special!

After getting back to Berk and Doris's apartment in Victoria, I continued my celebrations. Off I went to Barb and Ralph's on New Year's Eve to stay overnight for a big New Year's Day family turkey dinner. It was a surprise when my friend informed me that I was staying over a second night, as we were invited to another old friend's for dinner on January 2.

For someone who expected to be lonely during Christmas, I had a spectacular two weeks of celebrating the season. It was one of my most memorable since I became a solo traveller of life. While I missed my family, I had chosen to live life intentionally and focus on the positive aspects of the world around me. It was much better than wallowing in loneliness. It was a perfect Christmas!

The horse and buggy ride and the tuba band were great fun in Victoria

Life Long Learning

*Most people want to hear a good story. But they don't realize they can and should **BE** a good story. That requires intentional living.*

~ *John Maxwell*

Now that I was in Victoria, what to do? Do I sit back in a rocking chair and just speculate on how far I had come? Not on your life! I was ready for the next adventure.

I love September! All the college, university, and local community centres have their course selections out for the fall. I can sit down with a cup of tea and plan what I'm going to learn this winter.

My commitment to lifelong learning that began in the '90s continued. Now I was addicted to it! I loved to learn something new and hoped I would keep that attitude until I keeled over. Life was too fascinating to just sit back and vegetate!

The concept of *lifelong learning* was coined as long ago as 1970, but it became really popular in the '90s when I was fifty-seven. It came to international attention in research studies, as European and North American governments realized that to keep pace with the rapid advance of technology, their workforce also needed to continue learning or become redundant. At the beginning, lifelong learning was focused on economic outcomes, but as time progressed, people began to realize there was much more to it than that. Lifelong learning is defined as everything we learn throughout our lives from cradle to grave, from early childhood to the care and training of older workers.

It can happen in formal educational institutions, community centres, or union centres. It can include vocational skills in the workplace that lead to diplomas or certificates. Learning also happens in informal settings, such as our daily life activities related to our families. I didn't realize this until I went back to get my grade twelve diploma and got credits for life experience. I also found that my brain was more receptive to learn when I went back to school in mid-life. My focus was different than it was when I was a teenager.

Society used to think that once we finished formal education, we were done with school and we just got on with the business of working and living life. But technology began to advance rapidly—not every six years, but every few months. At seventy, I thought back on all the firsts I'd seen in my life. I'd seen type-writers become computers, and computers become tablets; cell phones went from huge monstrosities to ones that fit in the palm of your hand, and people text or email now instead of writing a letter or faxing a document. In the face of such rapid change, governments and educators had to convince workers that to continue learning was an essential part of their working life, or they would soon be redundant in the workplace. As the job markets became more competitive, lifelong learning helped people keep up with the latest technology.

As this concept advanced, universities conducted studies on the benefits of lifelong learning, and surprising results were revealed. There were obvious socio-economic advantages to the investment in human capital, which benefitted society as a whole. Researchers discovered there were many personal benefits when a person was committed to lifelong learning. It not only sharpens a person's confidence and interpersonal skills, but it also sharpens the mind, as I'd already learned in Dr. Oz and Dr. Roizen's book.

A Mayo Clinic study states, "Cognitive vitality is essential to the quality of life and survival in old age. Cognitive decline is clearly not inevitable. Human studies suggest that lifelong learning, mental and physical exercise, continuing social engagement, stress reduction, and proper nutrition may be important factors in promoting cognitive vitality in aging. There are various therapeutics, including cognitive enhancers and protective agents such as antioxidants and anti-inflammatories, which may prove useful and adjunct for the prevention and treatment of cognitive decline with aging."

My own commitment to lifelong learning meant that I wasn't just planning on sitting on one of those wonderful benches in Victoria and watching the world go by. I was going back to school. Again!

In my early life, I really liked to plan ahead. For the past twenty-five years leading a solo life, I have slowly become a person living by faith. I still sometimes like to plan things out so I'm not overwhelmed by surprising situations. Even when I drive a car, I don't want to be too close to the cars in front of me, preferring to use defensive driving techniques behind the wheel. I like to be in control of my environment, but God has called me to a different path. People asked how I could come back to Canada and not know where I was going to live. It wasn't always easy, because I still wanted to peek around the corner and see what was up ahead.

I prayed for direction from God, but many times if He didn't answer in the way I wanted, I might have thought He didn't answer prayers. But from past experience, I have found the answer could be yes, no, or wait. A delay in receiving an answer is just as much an answer as when fulfilment of the prayer comes. But I was impatient! Like many people, I found it hard to wait, yet I knew that it is in the faithfulness of waiting on God's answer that we grow in the knowledge of God. Many times, God's timing had been much better than mine.

"Everything is possible for one who believes." —Mark 9:23

The God of the universe held my life in His hands and had proved over and over again that I could trust Him. I think the most important things in this world are relationships, with God and with people.

The first year back in Canada was amazing! Once I arrived in Canada, I was immediately able to stay with my dear friend, Andrea, in Abbotsford while I figured out where to live permanently. Then that surprising opportunity opened up for me to house-sit Berk and Doris's apartment on Dallas Road while they went to the Philippines for six months. I enjoyed the seascape outside my window every day, especially during the storms that swept in from the ocean. Getting that apartment was an answer to prayer. It materialized after I had run around on my own strength searching the Victoria area.

The apartment was a place with no TV, which motivated me to focus on my writing. I found a writing group that met weekly, and this again inspired me to write more. Picking up the local *James Bay Beacon* newspaper one day, I noticed a large ad on the back page asking for volunteers to do layout for the newspaper. Right up my alley! My training was in desktop publishing, so I volunteered and found a great group of people to work with. Again, more motivation to write! I became very active volunteering in my community with the newspaper, serving lunches weekly to a seniors' group, making desserts for them, and doing the layout for the church photo directory. In a very short time, I got to know my community and made some great friends. A year before, I had no idea where I would live and only knew a few people in British Columbia. I trusted God to guide my steps, and He had opened up a whole new life to me … even at seventy-one.

On a lazy afternoon in July of that same year, I was crossing to Thetis Island on the ferry with my friend Andrea. We were on our way to a much-needed rest week at Capernwray Harbour Bible School. Andrea was another one of those encouragers in my life. As I enjoyed the sun and sea breeze, white puffy clouds skittered across the sapphire-blue sky. Still searching for what course to take in September, I casually stated to Andrea that if I were younger, I would love to go to Bible school.

She turned to me and said, "Why not?"

I was shocked! She had to be joking!

Andrea continued, "You're just like a college student right now. You have no home, no furniture, no commitments, and you're seeking God's direction for your life going forward."

Wow! I stood at the rail in stunned silence. Could it be possible? I definitely was seeking God's direction as to where to live in retirement, and for a purpose in life. I was opposed to being an inactive senior as I aged. My grandmother lived to ninety-seven, and I'm aiming at a hundred. That gave me about thirty years, which I thought God could put to use.

We had a wonderful week at Capernwray enjoying the sunshine and relaxing while being immersed in God's Word during the session times. I mentioned my desire to one of the staff responsible for registration, and she told me there was another seventy-year-old lady registered for the current session. I also spoke to a couple living on the grounds that had sold their property upon retirement and came to the school for a year. So I guess my desire wasn't so unique. The school found it a benefit to have mature students as part of the student body. I was considering school at seventy-one years of age! Given my history, I guess it wasn't really a surprise at this point.

In November of 2014, I went to experience a "Taste and See" week at the school. I was immersed in a week of being a part of the school to see if I would like it. After breakfast in the dining room, we headed up to the lecture hall to listen to a speaker on one book of the Bible. It was like a history lesson unfolded before me. After a great lunch of homemade soup and bread, I had the afternoon to roam the property and enjoy the beautiful gardens. After supper in the evening there was another lecture, and then the students had a game of indoor floor hockey. I loved it! The week I came back to the city seemed so dull after being with a group of students under twenty-five, with something going on every day. It felt right to consider school again!

September 2015, I went to live at Capernwray Harbour Bible School on Thetis Island to be immersed in Bible study for eight months. People asked me why I would want to do this at seventy-one. My answer was, "Why not?" I'm committed to lifelong learning, and I had an amazing opportunity open up before me. I just had to step through the door.

Wanting to be active and learning right to the end, I'm curious as to what adventure God has before me. So I decided to be still and trust that the God of the universe knows what my future will be, and it will be okay. I never dreamed a year before that God would open up a place to live, present me with new friends, and now an opportunity to go to Bible school at my age. Some people think that when they retire it's the end of an active life. I haven't found that to be true in my life. It's a choice!

Ponderings on School at Seventy-Two

If you aren't in over your head, how do you know how tall you are?

~ T.S. Elliot

I sat at my desk, looking out the window on the glass-calm waters of the Stuart Channel, just off the Strait of Georgia, in front of Thetis Island, BC. Little sparrows flitted around the tree just outside my window as the sun shimmered over the water. The water looked like a sea of diamonds. It was a peaceful moment as I pondered what I'd learned these first few weeks of being back at school as a mature student of seventy-two. My new buddy and hall mate, Rita, myself, and two other ladies were the only "mature" students with the rest of the one hundred student body under the age of twenty-five.

Rita was also my age, and we clicked like two peas in a pod. It felt like I'd known her for years. Rita is a tall, elegant lady with beautiful white hair, a gentle soul, and a solid faith walk. In the afternoons when we had free time, Rita and I would go for walks around the property to get our exercise and enjoy the gardens.

I thought I would feel the generational separation that seniors usually feel in a group of young people, but it was very different with this group.

Rita and I at Capenwray Bible School, Thetis Island, BC in 2015

It's strange to remember that when I was the age of these students, I was married with a child. Almost from day one, certain students gravitated toward the two of us. Some would just sidle up beside us and start a casual conversation, and others would ask what we thought of the book we had just read or the last lecture. They were curious why we would want to come to school at our age, and how many children and grandchildren we had. They were also fascinated that we both sold our homes and all our belongings before coming to school. Some shared problems they were working through, and we would pray. We couldn't do all the physical activity they could, and we didn't try. We were the cheering section during the team initiatives on the activity course at the beginning of the year.

Later when we went on a weekend venture hiking Mount Washington, the whole group helped us over slippery roots and puddles, and we all kept together as a team. Interaction with the other students has been refreshing regardless of the age. I missed all that stimulation later when I went home.

Age got us some bonuses. While the other students lived with up to five in a cottage, Rita, myself, and another mature student were in cozy rooms above the dining room of the main building. I watched the ferry come and go from my window looking out to the Stuart Chanel, and the tree outside my window was always full of birds flitting around.

Each student had a daily chore of about forty-five minutes, and ours had been adjusted to our age capabilities. The school has its own laying chickens, so for the first three weeks, Rita and I were on egg washing detail together. After that, I was on the veggie prep group after breakfast, making up veggie trays to go on every lunch table. Other students might wash dishes after meals, serve at meals, or clean their cabin or the general student areas. There was a pride in the students to keep their environment clean and tidy. This was probably a new concept for some. The school wasn't just training the students in the Bible—they were training them to be active, responsible participants in life.

My day began with breakfast at 7:45 a.m. I had veggie prep right after breakfast, with class starting at 9:15 a.m. Days were packed full! The morning lecture went until noon with a short break. Lecturers came from all over North America. One of my favourites, Bruce Campbell, came from Washington, USA, and the lecturer the following week was a Messianic Jew from Montreal who taught us the Life of the Messiah from the Jewish Perspective. Very enlightening! There was always something to challenge my mind and spirit. The teachers all linked the Old Testament to the New. The Old Testament is Christ concealed, and the New Testament is Christ revealed. It isn't a dry, boring book anymore; it's like an adventure book coming alive before my eyes.

Of course, God also used those times to challenge me too. I've been challenged to give up more of my self-will and independence to let God work through me. We read two books about what the life of a surrendered Christian really means. I had to ask myself if I only followed God for what He could provide in my life. Did I just follow the traditions of my "religion" by rote in the beautiful, stained glass windowed church? Was I just doing the "religious thing," or was I allowing Christ to work through my life? I pondered! What kind of Christian had I been up to that point? What did I want to be going forward?

When the lunch bell rang, it was a rush of one hundred students to sit down, with lots of noisy chatter. The meals were very good there, and lunch was usually homemade bread, veggie platters, and homemade soup. The mix was always changing and nutritious. Rita had egg washing after lunch, but otherwise the two of us were free to nap or catch up on our notes in the afternoon. When it started getting dark by the evening class, we tried to fit in a good half hour walk in the afternoon. The scenery there was very pastoral, with cows in two fields, and chickens behind the barn. One day Smoochie, the llama, squeezed under the fence, and it took a group effort to get him back in the pasture with the cows. One morning when I was walking up to the lecture hall to do my Internet time, one of the young cows had escaped. All the other cows were lined up at the fence, mooing at it. I could almost imagine them saying in cow talk, "Get your butt back in here." It was quite funny!

Supper was at 5:45 p.m., and the evening session went from 7:15 to 8:30 p.m. The bulk of the students weren't finished with their day until curfew at 10:30 and lights out at 11:00. The school was great to provide activity for them during the evening. There were hockey games, volleyball tournaments, various game nights, and campfires when the weather permitted. Rita and I didn't feel a need to be involved in the extracurricular activities after evening lecture. We were tired out by then and retreated to our rooms for tea and a chat.

Wednesday was work day. Everyone had a job for the day to keep the grounds beautiful and spotless. Rita and I were in the laundry but got to quit early as our energy ran out at our age. An afternoon nap was essential if we were to stay awake for the evening session. It was good to have an active day once a week rather than sit in class all the time. Also, some of these students had never experienced working like this and were learning new work skills.

At the end of the week we had to summarize, and hand in for marking, three to four pages of a journal on what we had learned that week. There were no exams, so the journal was the testing vehicle to be sure we understood what was being taught. If not, there was a staff person to come alongside any student who was struggling. No one slips through the cracks this way. Numerous times I would see a mentor or the lecturer sitting with a student to help them with their journal or to understand the day's lecture.

Sunday everyone leaves the island to go to one of the community churches. We were encouraged to try a few at the beginning of the year and then settle on one for the year. Supper on Sunday night was a formal affair with the men wearing dress pants, shirts, and ties, and the women wearing skirts or dresses to supper and the evening session. The staff served supper, and the tables were set with linen tablecloths, a special meal, dessert, and after dinner mints. One night there was a roast beef dinner with roast potatoes and veggies, finishing with flapper pie. Yum! The cook always made this a special meal.

Sunday evening service was my favourite! It started with a long time of praise music, and if you've never heard a hundred students singing, you've missed a special treat. It was amazing to see young people share what they had learned that week. If this energy was ever in all our home churches, there would be a revival spreading across Canada. It blessed my soul to see these young people every Sunday evening.

My time at Capernwray Harbour Bible School was challenging daily, and I had no idea what life would be like when I finished. But that was okay. God had a plan for my life, even at seventy-two years old.

Jeremiah 29:11 – "For I know the plans I have for you,' declares the LORD, 'plans to prosper you and not to harm you, plans to give you hope and a future.'"

Four mature ladies who went back to school with main dining hall in background.

Christmas Prep at School

An unintentional life accepts everything and does nothing. An intentional life embraces only the things that will add to the mission of significance.

~ John Maxwell

It was an amazing semester as a seventy-two-year old student in the midst of one hundred young adults in their late teens to early twenties! There had been speakers on everything from studying the book of Job with a pastor who was previously a trucker, to a Messianic Jew from Montreal teaching us about the Messiah from the Jewish perspective, then to a former addict teaching on the many forms of addiction, from drugs to cell phones. All lecturers were challenging to my understanding of the Bible, and also challenging to my spirit. I could see that God was more concerned with my availability than with my abilities. The world looks at our abilities and what we can do for them. It was a new concept for me that God just wanted me to be available to whatever He put in front of me. Taking good lecture notes felt less important than taking it all in. More thoughts to ponder on my upcoming break. The events of the last two weeks of the year at school were filled with busyness and excitement.

When I asked my son what he thought of me going to Bible school, he jokingly said, "Well, you were always a fanatic. What's the difference?" I knew he was joking, and I took it with a grain of salt. My daughters said, "Good for you, Mom!" Since I went to school for me, their evaluation was encouraging, but not necessary, for me to move forward. A big change from thirty years ago!

The ferry lights pierced through the darkness on the Stuart Channel, just off the Strait of Georgia as the ferry came into the Capernwray dock on Thetis Island. It was 8:30 p.m. in late November as students piled out of the lecture hall on our way to the dining hall. Excitement was in the air! There was a clear, full moon shining down on the pathway of scurrying students. We were all excited about the event! Many were dressed up in their fun Christmas attire as we neared the dining hall with anticipation.

The doors were flung open, and three staff members stood there to funnel us through the sunroom to the front of the building for the countdown of the lighting of the lights. Zinger, the cook, was there with his ho ... ho ... ho ... Santa sweater, Miriam was decked out in a snowman sweater, and Melody looked like a Christmas elf with her red and green combination. They were cheerful greeters to a night of Christmas fun.

Three ... two ... one ... and a cheer went up! Gaily coloured lights came on outlining the dining hall, bushes, and pump house, twinkling everywhere and making it look magical.

Afterward, one hundred students piled into the dining rooms, where tables were set up with bowls of M&Ms, pretzel sticks, and a huge array of candy for us to create and decorate our very own gingerbread house out of graham wafers. Hot apple cider and mandarin oranges were enjoyed by all as we built our special creations. There were many variations of the gingerbread house, from icing sandwiches to cabins with candy and marshmallow roofs. It was a fun night, followed in a week's time by another, more exciting, event to prepare for!

On the ninth of December, it was the night before one hundred students left Thetis Island for Christmas break. Bags were packed with care and ready to go on the first ferry the following morning. Excitement was in the air as students anticipated seeing their families again. But it was time to dress up one last time for the Christmas banquet and party in the lecture hall. Special cooking has been going on all week, tables moved and decorations up for the gala event. Prom dresses, mailed from home, were in evidence, and men were dressed in their suits and ties.

Rita and I wore long skirts and fancy tops, as most of our belongings were still packed away. No prom dresses for us! I really don't like large crowds, so I wasn't sure how long I'd last in the noise and crush. "Rita, if I disappear tonight, I'm okay," I said. "I can only take so much of crowds before I need to go back to the quiet of our rooms. Don't worry!" Knowing my dislike of large crowds, Rita just smiled. When I did disappear from the party, and someone asked where I was, Rita just told them I was okay and had slipped away for a while. What a good friend.

As we entered the lecture hall, we saw a tower of wine glasses with sparling apple juice in the middle of the foyer that reminded me of the cruise ship presentation when I had come from Florida to Vancouver the year before. Coats were taken and hung up by the staff as students are welcomed into the building and handed a glass from the tower. Much work had gone into the event by staff to make it a special night for the students. There was a dessert table in one corner, a coffee specialty bar in another, and staff mingling around the room with hors d'oeuvres. When the buffet opened, the food was beautifully displayed and delicious to enjoy. It was a special night and a great way to end the first semester of school. Even when I was immersed in learning, there needed to be some fun times to keep my life balanced.

The next morning, after grabbing a granola bar and some fruit in the dining room, we were all off to the first ferry of the day at 6:15 a.m. There was a long string of sleepy students walking down the path to the ferry, dragging suitcases and backpacks behind them, for the three-quarter-of-an-hour ferry ride. Arriving in Chemainus, we boarded the buses that would take us either to another ferry to the mainland and Vancouver airport, or down to Victoria airport. It was time for the rest and relaxation to begin.

As we approached Victoria along Highway One, Rita and I noticed that the area was experiencing a wind storm. On either side of the bus we could see the huge Douglas fir trees waving like flags in the wind. I thought it must be strong winds to move those tall trees, and it felt like our bus was the only safe place to be. With bits of branches flinging themselves against the bus, we rolled into Victoria. After arriving, the worst of the storm had passed, but I learned that the winds had been 100 to 114 km per hour, making them just shy of hurricane strength. Twenty thousand on Vancouver Island lost power in the storm. I thought about the emotional and physical storms in my life. Going through them was horrendous, but afterword I became stronger, the calm peace returned, and sun came out in my life. There were many lessons learned from observing nature around me.

The storms of my life had pummelled me at times. There was emotional debris scattered all around me, but I had faith there was an end to it and then the sun would come out. After the storm, all the debris was cleaned up, and you would never know there was a storm. I'm sure people looking at my life today couldn't imagine the storms of adversity it took to get to this point.

Since I had given up my place at Berk and Doris's apartment on the ocean to go to school, Rita and I stayed at a hotel in Victoria near the legislature buildings for a bit, before we both headed in different directions for the holiday. We spent the following week enjoying the Christmas lights and festivities, including the tuba concert in Market Square and a Messiah concert at Alix Goolden Performance Hall. Victoria, and particularly James Bay, is my favourite place in Canada, especially during this season. Spending time with my church family at Church of Our Lord was special before heading off to Langley to spend Christmas with Andrea and her family, my BC adopted family.

It was special to be spending time with family and friends over the Christmas season, but I couldn't wait to see what another semester of exploring and expanding my understanding of God's Word bring, and what His plan was for the next chapter of my life.

Where Does My Strength Come From?

Change can be difficult, but it becomes easier when you do it a little at a time. Success is gained in inches at a time, not miles.

~ John Maxwell

I had been praying as to where God wanted me to go for the school March break and also where I was to live once school was over. I sent emails as feelers out to mission organizations. Nothing materialized, but I knew that God had a plan for my life and I just had to wait. Waiting was the most difficult part for the planner in me, but God had been teaching me to trust Him for my future, and waiting had been a big part of that!

On January 28, 2015, I got an email from my past landlord's daughter, asking me to call her mother. I left a message on her phone and later, when I saw I'd missed a call from her, I didn't listen to the message before I called her back. She had an empty apartment for March 1 and wanted to know if I wanted it. I told her I wasn't finished school until May, so we ended the call. Later I listened to the voice message and discovered that the lady vacating the apartment wanted to sell all her solid oak furniture for $500. This would not only give me a place to live after school, but also provide a place to go in March. I called back that evening and the landlady said there were two other people who wanted the apartment, but she would do her best to stop everything for me. The next day she called back to say that the apartment was mine.

"Cast all your anxiety on Him, because He cares for you."
I Peter 5:7

In February my son called from Ontario to say that my granddaughter was being flown out to Victoria the Sunday night after my Mission Fest event to check out the University of Victoria (UVic). UVic was courting my granddaughter, so I had two days alone with my son while his daughter checked out the university. We walked all over Victoria, and we talked. This turned out to be a real blessing, as I hadn't seen him in three years, and he'd been having struggles in his life. It was some of the most honest conversation we'd had in years, and he now understands what I went through when my marriage split up. It was a special time! He fell in love with Victoria too and said he'd be back. Later, my granddaughter decided that UVic was where she wanted to go for her four to five years of university, meaning I would get to see my family more often, which addressed my biggest concern about retiring in Victoria. I didn't know that my granddaughter would choose UVic when I came to consider retirement in Victoria in 2014. Nor had I ever considered that I would be going to Bible school.

During March break, I settled into my lovely, new, furnished apartment with oak furniture in perfect condition. The landlady wanted to make sure I was comfortable, so she loaned me sheets, towels, lights, etc. until I had time to purchase what I needed. There hadn't been an empty apartment in this building for five or six years. I felt very blessed to have gotten this wonderful furnished apartment for such a reasonable cost.

In April, the school year at Capernwray was almost over, and I was looking forward to returning to my church and all my friends in Victoria. For now, though, our final project was on the character of God, and my assignment was on El Shaddai. I didn't realize before that the many different names of God show His character, and I found it quite fascinating. We don't see the word "El Shaddai" in our Bible, but it's in the original Hebrew.

El Shaddai means God Almighty, the ALL Sufficient One.

El means God in Hebrew.

Shaddai means breasted; one that pours forth life, and it instills the image to me of a nursing mother that provides life-giving sustenance to a child.

God is the One Who is Almighty; "all powerful" to nourish, supply and satisfy in all we do, say, and be when He is the One Who is living in and through us! He is the Bread of Life who strengthens and comforts.

I questioned myself: Do I think God can be my El Shaddai in today's world, or is the Bible full of stories that do not apply to my life today? Can God be trusted to be my El Shaddai, my all sufficient one?

> **"Whoever dwells in the shelter of the Most High will abide in the shadow of the Almighty [El Shaddai]. I will say to the LORD, 'He is my refuge and my fortress, My God, in whom I trust.'"**
> **Psalm 91:1–2,**

God knew the plan He had for my life! When I walked in God's way and stayed close to Him, no matter what I went through, He was faithful to be by my side. God never promised me a rose garden, but He promised to always be with me. I have found Him to be faithful and true! God is my El Shaddai, who nourishes, supplies, and satisfies in all I do, say, and be. He is the Bread of my life who strengthens and comforts me each day.

For the past twenty-five years as a solo traveller of life, I have truly known God as my El Shaddai, over and over again. Some people would call it coincidence, but I see God's hand providing for me. Other people say I have incredibly good luck, but I am confident that El Shaddai is alive and well in our world today when we trust Him completely with the direction of our lives.

Trusting isn't always easy. For many years I believed my faith walk was like a sailboat. If I stayed chained up to the dock of my old insecurities, I was safe but went nowhere. If I released the cords that tied me down and moved forward, God was the wind in my sails that would guide me where I need to go—even if I started out in the wrong direction. It's an image that has stuck with me for many years. God is the one who healed me and gave me courage to try the impossible. Now I considered what lay ahead and pondered again if I could trust God to direct my sails as I stepped into the excitement of graduation prep.

In May, the cherry blossoms were in bloom, white tents were put up on the lawns in case of rain, parents came from all over to witness their students graduating from Bible school, and in the kitchen, many delicious treats had been cooked up. Since my family was on the other side of Canada, my friend Andrea came over from the mainland to be my support during this special time of putting another brick in the foundation of confidence and following that thread of knowledge again.

Rita's family had also adopted me and were there rooting for me. It was another special graduation, the third in the last thirty years. Students were dressed in their Sunday best, with many smiles and cheerful chatting. We all filed into the front of the auditorium to receive our diplomas. Flash bulbs weren't crackling and popping this time like my previous two graduations, as we were now into the digital age, but many photos were still taken of proud graduates. After the ceremony, we enjoyed a lovely display of delicious food as students and family gathered on the patio under umbrella tables to enjoy the feast. Then the whole student body with suitcases in tow headed home on the last ferry ride they would take from Capernwray for a while. Many would come back over the years for visits, including myself.

When I got back to Victoria, Andrea helped me move my belongings into the new apartment, where another chapter began. I had finally decided that Victoria was definitely the place I wanted to retire, and I looked forward to this new adventure in my life. I LOVE Victoria!

This was not the end of the story. The adventure would continue one step at a time. The future was unknown, but the potential unlimited.

Rita and I at graduation with the whole body of students for the 2015/16 year.

Afterword: What Now at Seventy-Five?

> *The righteous will flourish like the palm tree; they will grow like*
> *a cedar in Lebanon. Planted in the house of the LORD, they will*
> *flourish in the courts of our God. They will still bear fruit in old age;*
> *they will stay fresh and green, proclaiming "The LORD is upright;*
> ***He is my rock!***
>
> ~ *Psalm 92:12–15,*

The journey of the last thirty years has been quite an adventure! It wasn't something I mapped out at the beginning and then just started ticking off each event when accomplished. They were short dreams of the next step, and then the next, and again the next. Each event built confidence in me. Sometimes my dreams were smashed to smithereens; other times they propelled me forward. The trick was that I never gave up and just kept moving forward. Tenacity is the key to long term dreams.

Now at seventy-five, I have incredible peace in my life. I love where I live, and I love my life. There were sacrifices along the way, failed marriages that I regret but know I wouldn't be the woman I am today if I had stayed. There would have been the comfort of family living close by, but now they come to visit me in my wonderful retirement dream place. When a person has such a dramatic paradigm shift in life, there are always sacrifices, but the rewards are usually greater. I'm still a person of strong faith in the creator of the universe; actually, my faith has become stronger through it all. That has been the healing in my life and the thing to keep me positive on this journey. The Lord has definitely been the rock in my life as I have travelled.

For two years, until 2017, I lived in the lovely furnished apartment in James Bay after school at Capernwray. My name finally came up for a geared-to-income apartment at a Baptist housing complex I'd applied for when I first came to British Columbia in 2014. There are two independent buildings where I live, two assisted living buildings, and a high-end seniors building. Now I can age in place independently where I am, confident that my little savings will last me as long as I need them to. If I ever need to be in an assisted living situation, I'll be able to move over to one of the other buildings. It's a safe environment for my senior years with lots of activity going on right in the complex if I want to be involved. But that doesn't mean I'm sitting in a rocking chair like a shmuck. I want to keep active till I keel over.

One night many years ago, just after my divorce, I had a dream that was so vivid, I had to get up and type it out. I didn't know what the dream meant until now, many years after the dream. Here is the dream I called "Jewels in Destruction."

> *I dreamt that I was on a hillside overlooking a city.*
> *Behind me were the offices of the people responsible*
> *for coordinating a huge reconstruction of the city*
> *below. The city was on the edge of a large body of*

water. I was being brought into the construction office as an expert.

Below, the landscape of the city was block after block of demolished buildings. Bricks and rubble were everywhere! Large steam shovels were scooping up the rubble and filling truck after truck with the debris, which was then hauled off. On the far right, some old buildings were left standing, but the exterior was being painted a pure and gleaming white.

As I walked toward my new office, I noticed used office equipment lying neatly in various piles beside the pathway. When I asked the construction foreman what the office equipment was doing there, he told me that they were materials left behind by the people as they moved out of the demolished buildings below. The workmen had recovered the good and usable articles from the buildings before they were demolished. The articles were put by the path for anyone to take what they could use.

Since I was setting up a new office to supervise the demolition and re-construction of the city, I picked up the useful materials to accomplish this. Soon I was picking up more than I could use and giving it to other people who could put it to good use. Soon the articles along the path turned into beautiful gold accessories for a home or office, and some expensive clothing that was just my size. Again I started giving the excess to others. Everything that I needed for *setting up my new office as the coordinator of the re-construction of the city was found on the pathway.*

Somehow, I could sense that whatever I would need to create the new city would come from the old. The useable, practical, beautiful, and quality articles were being taken from the old to help create the new. The old, dilapidated, and un-useful was being torn down, sorted, and hauled away by the trucks. I sensed this was a healthy process. The old and decaying buildings would be replaced by new, bright buildings, but that which was of value from old buildings would be retained and used or shared with others.

What did it mean? It was a question I had for many years until I realized that the dream was prophetic. The city was of course my life, and I did pick up the good from my old shattered life that would create a new and good life, despite what I had lost. Looking back now, I can see how, over the years, I had taken the good from my previous life to create a new, better me. Growth at times was painful, but the end result was gratifying.

Still involved in volunteer work outside of where I live, I keep involved in my community with a number of activities. There is layout and being on the Board of Directors of a local newspaper, filling in for the church receptionist when he goes on holiday, helping serve at various dinners or tea events, and doing a monthly newsletter for Baptist Housing. At seventy-four, for the first time in my life, I took up watercolour painting on Japanese art paper from a talented teacher, Richard Wong, and loved it. At seventy-five, I even had three paintings in a gallery for emerging artists.

What next? Well, I'm thinking of taking English classes at the university that is close to me in September. I said many times earlier that I want to be the little old lady in running shoes travelling down the university hallways as long as I can. Of course, publishing this book at seventy-five is also a goal this year, as is setting up a web page to sell my paintings and art cards. Recently, someone asked me if I would do travel writing of Vancouver Island for a new business web page. Maybe I will.

Life is too precious to just sit and vegetate. I plan to enjoy every minute until my time is done. I'm aiming at a hundred, so I have to be sure to eat well, walk lots, and keep my mind active to get there in good form. One of my other goals is to travel the Inside Passage up the West Coast of Canada again and write another book about it. So stay tuned!

*This is my vision of retirement: family, travel, friends,
and God as my strength and refuge.*

Lessons of Life to Inspire

Significance is usually not a result of anything spectacular. It's based on small steps in line with purpose.

~ John Maxwell

What is growth? Growth is not just going to school, reading, or academic advancement. It's an all-encompassing philosophy that involves mind, body, spirit, and psyche. I develop my mind by always being ready to learn something new each day, whether in a lecture, reading a book, observing nature and human nature, or studying to learn a new subject at school. At forty-six I took that plunge into a three-year college degree and discovered I had a brain in my head that had not gone to mush. I found me! In the process, I lost my fear and gained the confidence to speak my mind regardless of what others thought. I realized I had an analytical mind; they were my thoughts, and I was entitled to them. I became brave in expressing myself!

I developed my body by getting in touch with what is happening to it. Learning to eat what is healthy for my body and balancing a reasonable amount of exercise to reduce the stress in life helps me to keep chugging along to the best of my ability. I no longer leave the care and destiny of my body to other people. That's my responsibility! I've had to adjust my eating many times over the years because of health issues, but I'm healthier today than I was at thirty. I try to walk eight thousand steps a day. I don't always make it, but it's my goal and I always feel better for it. Life in the middle doesn't mean that your best years are past; the best can be just ahead.

How do I develop my spirit? The changes in my life you've been reading about happened after I developed a faith in the God of the universe and His Son, who redeemed my soul. I began to grow after my faith became real. I continue to develop and grow in that faith as I nurture it with study, worship, and fellowship with other believers. I search for heroes as role models of life. One of my current role models is a ninety-seven-year-old lady who still goes downtown on the bus by herself. I want to be like her with a positive attitude at ninety-seven. God has eradicated the fear and depression from me. I have learned to speak in front of others, or cook for large groups, without ending up with my stomach in knots and a blinding headache. I'm no longer afraid to step out and do whatever I want in life. It's liberating!

I develop my psyche by learning more about who I am each day, with all the bumps and warts. As I learn more about who I am as a person, I try not only to accept the creation that God has made, but also to see the part that needs work. With God's help each day I try to change the negative parts of my personality. I fail a lot of the time, but I keep trying and striving for the ultimate goal. No matter what my age, I hope to keep being a better me.

Growth, to me, is a living, fluid organism that ebbs and flows like the ocean tide. At times I grow in great leaps and then flow along as I assimilate new information. Sometimes I feel the undertow that seems to suck me backwards, but growth is always moving, and soon it rushes in with another cresting wave. To stop growing is to become dull and stagnant. If I live to be a hundred, I hope to be growing and learning something new about myself and the world around me to the very end. Growth is living life on purpose. Life is too short and valuable to waste.

There's too much to experience to sit on the sidelines waiting for someone to make decisions for me or change their view to mine, or to wait until others accept or reject me because my view is different from theirs. Life is but a mist ... here today and gone tomorrow. What is lasting? The relationships that I develop with people are the only things people will remember. I can't develop relationships sitting in a box, or by not being true to my own feelings. I own only who I am, and if I'm not true to that, then I have nothing to offer others. I can't touch others' lives without growing myself.

I keep growing my mind by being a lifelong learner. Teaching others a craft or what life has taught will not only help the next generation, but will regenerate my mind at the same time. Life is precious. I seek to exercise my brain muscle so that I can enjoy future generations. Right now, I'm learning to write a book and create with watercolour painting on Japanese art paper.

Now my passion in life is to encourage and motivate others to dream new dreams, to dare to push beyond their comfort zone and experience life with new perspective. I want to challenge people to be aware of those they're in contact with each day, to give sincere appreciation and encouragement when they see an opportunity. One person's words may be the motivation to change another person's life. I spend time occasionally with my granddaughter, baking and trying to encourage her on her life journey. I think that's my job as a grandmother, to encourage and motivate my grandchildren to reach their potential. I've even learned to text so I can send little words of encouragement to them from time to time.

One person's words changed my life! I still remember the people in my life who were my encouragers over the past thirty years. First there was Jean Baker in my first English class, who asked me if I ever considered a career in writing. Then Don Baker, who hired me to promote the Adult Learner Program in which I was a student. Then the two teachers in that same program—Marilyn B, who taught me math, and Pat, who encouraged me to write. They were like my rooting team! Then when I went to Mohawk College there were a myriad of teachers that motivated me to go on and accepted me just for who I was, not who I was "supposed to be." That was a real paradigm shift in my life. After college I had many friends that encouraged me on my journey—people like Wendy and Eileen, who went through the tough times of my marriage and encouraged me where I was. Andrea in British Columbia gave me the opportunity to explore living in BC and encouraged me with this book.

There are so many people I've been blessed to have in my life these last thirty years that have been encouragers to motivate me forward, that I'm sure I would miss someone if I tried to list them all. And you would get bored reading them all. I list a few to show you the power of encouragement each of us can make in another's life.

My life has not been a bed of roses, but it has been an adventure. My faith has kept me strong and helped me through the tough times. I just kept walking through the next door that opened before me, and then the next, and the next. I continue to be a lifelong learner in the world around me.

My journey goes on ... and who knows where it will lead? At seventy-five, I'm aiming at a hundred. I will be that one-hundred-year-old shuffling down the halls in my new Nike runners to my next class, or discovering something new in travel. I will dream new dreams and look forward to meeting interesting people along the way. I discovered that success isn't about what we have or don't have; it's about what we do with what life gives us! I consider myself a blessed and successful person. Life is an adventure!

So are you ready to start your adventure? It starts with the first step.

For You: Steps to Making a Dream Reality

Go confidently in the direction of your dreams. Live the life you have imagined. Our truest life is when we are in dreams awake. Dreams are the touchstones of our character.

~ Henry David Thoreau

Do you have a dream? More education, better job, travel, start a business, or leave a bad situation? Do you feel life has passed you by and it's too late for you? You're too old? I want to assure you today that it's never too late to dream a dream and accomplish it, no matter how old you are. This section is all about you! How do you get unstuck, move forward, and accomplish your dream? No one can do it for you. It's all up to you, taking one step at a time. It took many years, but now I've grown into ownership of my own life, acting instead of reacting. I love life now!

Perhaps you think it will take too long. So what? Step by step, inch by inch, you can achieve anything you set your mind to. Walt Disney said, "If you can dream it, you can do it." If you never start out on a journey, you will never move from where you are now. But if you get to the end of the block, you're further along than you were yesterday. It matters not how long it takes; the process is what matters. So what is stopping you?

My motivation was that first night school class and seeing the possibility. I never dreamed then I would be where I am at seventy-five. The analogy I use for my life is the sailboat I talked about earlier. I chose to cast off from the dock and raise my sails, to let the wind fill those sails. Jesus is the wind in my sails that directs my life.

A dream can be something as unreal as the fantasies of sleep, or it can be the motivator from which truly great things are done. Webster's Thesaurus says that to dream is "to long, crave, hunger or thirst" for something. It says a dreamer is "a person whose conduct is guided more by ideals than practicalities." I believe there's a little bit of dreamer in each of us. The difference is whether we allow our dreams to take form.

One thing that helped me to let my dreams take form was to make a collage of what I thought my life would look like at a certain point in time. It started when I had a serious depression. I created my first collage to pull myself out of it by appreciating the positive things in my life. Since then, I've done two more collages: one for what self-employment would look like, and one for what retirement would look like. They hung on my walls for many years. Looking back on them now, I'm amazed to see that I've accomplished most of what I had on my story boards. Each picture represented a specific thing I wanted in my life.

Dreams, as opposed to fantasies, are the real fabric of our humanity. Explorers, scientists, and inventors all used dreams to their advantage.

How do you turn a dream into reality?

A. Focus

The first step is to distinguish the difference between a dream and a fantasy. What may be fantasy to one may, with great determination, be an attainable goal to another. How determined are you? Only you can answer this.

B. Aim at something

Dreams are essential to life! If you don't have a dream, then you aim at nothing. If you aim at nothing, you will hit your target every time. You become a victim of life, shifting with every wave of adversity. But if in aiming at a dream you hit below the mark, at least you've achieved more than you would have when aiming at nothing. So what have you got to lose? Nothing!

C. Visualize

Focus on the goal at the end and rip up a magazine to show pictures of what you're trying to achieve. After all, isn't that what an architect does when planning a new building? With each picture you pick, you're picking what you want in your life in the future.

D. Action plan

Write down a step-by-step list of what you need to do to start moving toward your dream. Do you need to find out if your board of education offers adult learner programs? In my county, upgrading to a grade twelve diploma was free. After all, you've been paying your taxes for education. Maybe it's post-secondary you want. Research your local colleges to see what courses are offered that interest you and if they give mature student credits. Some employers will give you time off on half days to upgrade your education, or even pay for you to upgrade your skills. It will benefit their company if you have more skills. Be single-minded in short-term steps toward your goal.

E. Share your plan

Share your plan with someone who cares about you. Our dreams come from the tender part of our heart, and we need the help of a trusted friend to connect our heart to our brain with practicality. Mind you, I said trusted! Some very well-meaning "friends" in this world have been known to crush a dream that had the potential of true genius. My husband's favourite joke when I was going to school was, "Behind every successful wife is a pushy husband." A true friend, and someone I did trust to encourage me in my plans!

F. Faith and courage

Now faith is confidence in what we hope for and assurance about what we do not see. —Hebrews 11:1
Dreams can get you through difficult times in life, because you always have hope of a better tomorrow. With faith and courage, you can realize your dream. Faith is like a parent's kind hand under you as you learn to swim. They said that you would swim if you trusted. So you did trust, even though you couldn't see the hand supporting you. You had faith in your parent. You may not know how you will realize your dream, but you know that each little step will get you closer to it.

G. Persevere

Dreams we develop into goals cause us to stretch and grow. Dreams have built nations, invented spectacular spacecraft, and written beautiful poetry. The path may not always be smooth, but never give up on your dreams. Readjust and strive on! Sometimes I wanted to pull the blankets over my head and shout, "Stop the world. I want to get off." Thankfully the feelings didn't last long, and life went on. I just kept trudging along!

Dreams are for everyone. To stop dreaming is like trying to stop participating in life.

I want to challenge you to write down your dream and the steps to make it happen. Grasp your dream, no matter how old you are, and you will feel the power of self-achievement. Enjoy the adventure!

What are your dreams? Where are you going? Who are you going to be? Make a plan and take the first step into your future!

H. Wise Words to Live By

Wise words have motivated me along in my journey and encouraged me when I was down.

I. You probably noticed my love for inspirational quotes, the ones I peppered throughout the book. Such words have been so meaningful and helpful to me, and so I end with a few more here for you:

> *The purpose of life is not to be happy. It is to be useful,*
> *to be honourable, to be compassionate, to have it make some*
> *difference that you have lived and lived well.*
> *~ Ralph Waldo Emerson*

Sometimes the smallest step in the right direction ends up being the biggest step in your life. Purpose is like a snowball rolling downhill... it builds over time.
~ John Maxwell

Be the change you want to see in the world.
~ Mahatma Gandhi

Our real freedom comes from being aware that we do not have to save the world, we must merely make a difference in the place we live.
~ Parker Palmer - philosopher

Acknowledgements

To all of those teachers who inspired me on this journey—Jean and Don Baker, Marylyn Bentley, Pat, to mention a few—I send out a big THANK YOU. I may never see you again, but you may read this book and realize you helped this one woman to change her life. The Halton Board of Continuing Education Adult Learner program started the process that became a paradigm shift in my life. I am forever indebted to the program as well as the people who ran it and created it. Thank you.

On my journey to investigate how to publish a book, I met Barbara Edie in Victoria at her book launch of *Creating the Impossible* (*www.barbaraedie.com*). Barbara is also a motivational writer, speaker, and coach who is living an intentional life and paying it forward to inspire others to live a life of purpose. Barbara encouraged me to publish and connected me to my amazing editor, Jen Violi (https://www.jenvioli.com). Jen is an affirmation guru who kept me focused to get through the fine tuning. I feel very blessed to have been recommended to her. Junie Swadran and Sheila Martindale, writing coaches, encouraged me to publish this book in the early stages of writing.

Wendy Martynuik, Eileen Moore Crispin, Andrea Soberg and Lii Vine, four of my long-time friends on this journey, read the rough draft and gave me positive input to move forward. All of these people, and too many to mention here, have inspired me to write my story to encourage others. Finally, my dear friend in BC, Rita Springer, gave me the final push, inspiration, and support to actually publish this book.

Winston Churchill said, "We make a living by what we get, but we make a life by what we give." I want to live a life intentionally that makes a difference in the world. There have been many people who have encouraged and motivated me along the journey. Many thanks to all those people who have encouraged me to finalize and publish this book. I hope it inspires you on your own journey to dream your dreams and achieve your goals, no matter how old you are. There were so many people who motivated and encouraged me on the journey that I'm sure I would miss someone if I tried to mention them all.

Life is a precious commodity. Enjoy the journey!

---

[i] Steven Covey, *Seven Habits of Highly Effective People* (New York: Free Press, 1989)

[ii] Anthony Campolo, The Power of Delusion (Wheaton, IL: Victor Books, 1983)

[iii] Dr. Mehmet Oz and Dr. Michael Roizen, *YOU: Staying Young* (New York: Scribner, 2007)

[iv] John Maxwell, *Intentional Living, Choosing a Life that Matters* (New York: Centre Street Publisher, 2015) All John Maxwell quotes come from this book

[v] 2002 Mayo Foundation for Medical Education & Research. Published by Elsevier, Inc. "Benefits of lifelong learning," *Procedia—Social & Behavioral Sciences* 46(2012) 4268–4272. Can Learn (2009) Continuing Education, Canada.

CPSIA information can be obtained
at www.ICGtesting.com
Printed in the USA
LVHW092241181019
634685LV00003B/4/P